T0146717

I Want to
Enjoy
My Children

Henry Brandt, Ph.D.
Kerry L. Skinner

MULTNOMAH
BOOKS

I WANT TO ENJOY MY CHILDREN

published by Multnomah Books
© 2002 by Dr. Henry Brandt and Kerry L. Skinner

International Standard Book Number: 978-1-57673-971-6

Cover image by V.C.L. / Getty Images

Unless otherwise indicated, Scripture quotations are from: *The Holy Bible,*
New King James Version © 1979, 1980, 1982, Thomas Nelson, Inc.

Other Scripture quotations: *The Holy Bible,* New International Version (NIV) © 1973, 1984
by International Bible Society, used by permission of Zondervan Publishing House

Published in the United States by WaterBrook Multnomah, an imprint of the Crown Publishing
Group, a division of Random House Inc., New York.

MULTNOMAH and its mountain colophon are registered trademarks of Random House Inc.

For information:
MULTNOMAH BOOKS
12265 Oracle Boulevard, Suite 200
Colorado Springs, CO 80921

Library of Congress Cataloging-in-Publication Data
Brandt, Henry R.
  I want to enjoy my children / by Henry Brandt and Kerry L. Skinner.
      p. cm.
Includes bibliographical references.
  ISBN 9781576739716(pbk.)
    1. Child rearing—Religious aspects—Christianity. I. Skinner, Kerry L., 1955– II. Title.
  BV4529 .B6794 2002
248.8'45—dc21

                                                                                          2001008466

146620572

TABLE OF CONTENTS

ACKNOWLEDGMENTS

To Kerry Skinner, who took my original manuscript and prepared it for publication. He is a good, trustworthy friend.

To Elaine Skinner, who read through the manuscript for us many times.

To Renee DeLoriea, for her wonderful work as an editor.

FOREWORD

I HAVE BEEN READING DR. HENRY BRANDT'S BOOKS SINCE he first began writing. Indeed, I have known his work much longer than I've known him personally.

More recently, to my great delight, we have become personal friends and professional colleagues. But my first impression has never changed.

In a culture that sometimes worships reeds, Henry Brandt is an oak tree. That doesn't mean he can't adjust and adapt. Oak trees spread their leaves and take in new rays of sunshine every day. The hardier varieties can even find refreshment in the winds of change.

But the roots of oak trees go deep and often cling to solid rock. Henry Brandt's bedrock has always been the same biblical values on which he founded his ministry in the first place. Dr. Brandt is a faithful, longtime student and practitioner of God's Word. I don't believe he has ever wavered in his devotion to the fundamental child-rearing principles first established by God, which are timeless and yet inherently modern in every sense.

Who could possibly understand children better than our Creator? And who could possibly advise parents with more confidence, sensitivity, and plain old understanding than one who studies, works, and writes in partnership with the author of all things?

Ironically, on a person-to-person level, many people now seem to know a lot more about parenting than we knew a few hundred years ago. After all, we've invented many new forms of raising children and studied them exhaustively. Dual parenting, single parenting, part-time parenting, absentee parenting—all these represent relatively new approaches to family life.

And yet God knows more about parenting than any of us. Dr. Henry Brandt rests firmly in that supreme knowledge and draws from it more effectively, more consistently, and more enthusiastically than anyone I know.

Dr. Brandt has another major contributor as well: Kerry Skinner, who organizes and writes with solid conviction and deft ability. What they have produced together is a book that will bless your life in every way.

You will enjoy encountering God's timeless truths through the eyes and heart of one of His most faithful servants.

DR. HENRY T. BLACKABY

PREFACE

I BELIEVE THAT MOST OF US WOULD LIKE TO BE DESCRIBED as George Eliot so powerfully states:

> Oh, the comfort, the inexpressible comfort, of feeling safe with a person. Having neither to weigh thoughts nor measure words, but pouring all right out just as they are, chaff and grain together, certain that a faithful friendly hand will take and sift them, keep what is worth keeping, and with a breath of understanding, blow the rest away.

What would a man give for a wife like that? Probably as much as a woman would give for such a husband.

When I was forty-four years old, Homer Dowdy and I wrote *Building a Christian Home*. At that time we said the trail was downhill when the family reaches the "empty nest" stage. But we were wrong. In fact, the trail got even steeper from there. Surprisingly, the steepest part came after we reached sixty.

However, at age seventy-six, the view from this elevation is magnificent—even though it was hard work getting here. Yes, the trail ahead is still steep, but now I can look back down the trail, all the way to the bottom. From here I can see people who are just beginning the climb. Some have started up the trail. If only they could see what I see, it would make a difference in how they prepare for the climb. My desire is to help you see from my vista so that you can be more prepared for the climb ahead. This is why I am now writing this book.

As I reflect on the elements of family living, a very special day comes to my mind. This particular memory is so significant to me because my friends and I had literally reached the top of a mountain after working together, laughing together, and suffering together through much hardship.

My three companions and I stood at the top of a glacier, astounded at the breathtaking view stretching out eight-thousand feet below us. There was a solemn quietness at the top of that mountain. What a thrill! What joy we experienced as we breathed in our sense of accomplishment, knowing that we had realized our goal. We stood speechless, drinking in the vastness of the wide world at our feet.

It had been an eight-hour climb over unfamiliar, rugged terrain. Poorly fitting shoes had caused several blisters. A fall that ended on a rock netted a painful bruise. One hand throbbed with pain because it had grabbed hold of a thorny branch. At one point we came to a sheer cliff and as a more experienced member of the party started up, we watched with uncertainty. Although loose boulders came hurtling past us and bounced down to the base of the mountain, our friend made it and we were encouraged to begin climbing again.

At another point in the climb there was a steep, snowy field to cross. Slipping and sliding made our hearts race wildly, and it took courage even to move. Then we came to long, shady trails that were lined with great timbers and covered with soft, cool moss. Swift, clear streams and lacy waterfalls were close by. At last we reached the summit—tired, aching, and hungry, but victorious and satisfied. It was worth the effort. We were happy.

Many people have looked up at those gleaming, snowcapped peaks and at that glacier, which seemed so near, so accessible, so inviting. Some have started out to conquer them, filled with enthusiasm and purpose, yet the climb upward filled them with fear. For them, the miles have been disappointing and disheartening. When they discovered the distance to be greater and the ascent to be much steeper than they had anticipated, the disheartened have become utterly unappreciative of the quiet valleys, the great trees, the roaring rapids, and the mighty waterfalls. Instead, these tentative climbers have become increasingly aware of tired muscles, sore feet, exhaustion, and dampness. Somewhere along the way, when they faced a particularly difficult grade, their courage faltered and their purpose died. Then, instead of reconsidering and taking heart in the goal, they gave up, turned around, and headed home—because they had been unprepared or unwilling to face the obstacles.

The successful climbers, on the other hand, have found pleasure and challenge in the very roughness and hardness of the journey. They have found joy in the same difficulties that overwhelmed others. The struggle up the mountain was rewarding, though exhausting. Success in mastering a slope inspired courage and hope for tackling the next one. Mountain climbing offers beautiful vistas, long periods of uninteresting and undesirable stretches, brisk air, steep and difficult places, danger, strain, pain…and cooperation. Mountain climbers depend on each other: They sustain, pull up, and boost each other. The demands of the climb and need for interdependence build a bond of friendship among some climbers—and breed conflicts among others.

This summit view affords an appraising look at marriage. All who marry start out together walking joyously, hand in hand, with high hopes, eagerly anticipating what is to come. Beckoning them up the trail is a life of establishing a home and raising a family. From their vantage point, it all seems so easy to attain, so inviting.

Marriage is not like walking along a familiar trail that you have explored many times and for which you know every twist and turn along the way. Marriage, rather, is more like a strange trail with every turn holding something new. There are some pleasant stretches that are easily mastered. Then, there are also steep, rugged places that leave the couple aching and exhausted. One fact in life is certain: the certainty of uncertainty. The mature Christian makes his way along the trail with keen interest, enjoying the variety and finding satisfaction in meeting the challenges of a new baby in the family, a promotion, moving to another house, sickness, death, accidents, or another kind of new chapter in life together. My wife and I have experienced all of these steep places and more. We hadn't expected all of them to happen to us.

We have found that each change, with the problems that it brings, exposes the soul. But the climber has this promise: "The humble He guides in justice, and the humble He teaches His way" (Psalm 25:9).

We have discovered that humble sojourners will gather the facts, sift them, and proceed according to God's way, but the hardships of the climb made us increasingly aware that we alone were not able to walk in love every step of the way. Praise God, however, we were never alone. It was His mercy that kept us reliant on Him, at each step realizing our need for God and His ways. Like you, we needed a Savior and access to the Spirit of God. And I can assure you that both were, and are, there for the asking.

We discovered that the "empty nest" mark is not the summit. We were surprised to find that several gleaming, snow-covered peaks were still ahead. In fact, the climb from the fifty-six-year-old mark to the seventy-six-year-old mark was the most painful, difficult, and demanding climb of them all. Ahead of us looks like another steep climb, and beyond that peak is eternity.

When we look down the trail, we can see some confusion and congestion. We see some people who do not seem to be able to decide if they are going to come up any higher or give up and go back down the slope. Some of them have turned around already. A few of them still have their faces pointed upward. The people on the trail who seem to be confused have the latest climbing clothes and equipment. They appear to be well fed. Below them are some bedazzling, brilliantly lit places. Those people who have started to head downward to the twinkling lights below have determined that the uphill trail is too narrow, stressful, and steep.

Although the appearance of ease and comfort looks appealing from a distance, retreat will always prove to be empty. The climber who gave up on making the ascension of God's pathway will always long for the journey that will take them to the top of the summit.

The purpose for writing this book is to encourage you to journey upward with joy on your face. Maybe you have turned around and started heading toward what you think might be an easier way. Or maybe you have lost heart, are overtaken by fear, and can't muster up the strength to go any higher. Or maybe you are moving upward, but you are not enjoying the journey. Whatever the case, I invite you to be comforted, be encouraged, and be courageous as you press into all that God has for you and for your family.

You may be a parent who has recently married and just started your family. Or you may be a single parent who is suddenly journeying without your spouse. Or you may be journeying with your children in a situation where you are remarried. Regardless of your marital status, I want to encourage you to journey upward, guiding your children up the slope as you all keep your eyes fixed on Jesus.

My friend, our hearts grieve for those people who will not see the trail from my vista unless they turn around and begin to head upward again. As I watch their backs, slumped downward in defeat as they give up, I want to yell after them: "Turn around, turn your gaze upward to Jesus Christ. Just take one step at a time, one moment at a time, relying on God, being renewed and strengthened in Him, and keep climbing the slope His way." I want to cry out to them: "Don't settle for less, for the idols of this world, because they are nothing more than a sham." I want to shout this Scripture to them: "'For what is a man profited if he gains the whole world, and loses his own soul?'" (Matthew 16:26).

If there is a single, major point in this book that we would like to put in blaring lights from our vista point, it is this: Be renewed day by day in:

- comfort and consolation—(see 2 Corinthians 1:3–5)
- patience and joy—(see Colossians 1:11)

- wisdom—(see James 1:5)
- righteousness—(see Philippians 3:9)
- peace and hope—(see Romans 15:13)

The serious Christian who recognizes his need of Christ as his Savior and as his source of renewed life will not be overwhelmed by the stresses and strains of the journey. You are not alone. You will have good success and fullness of journey if you lock arms with the Lord and don't look back.

CENTRALITY OF THE BIBLE

As you read this book, you will find that we will constantly be pointing you to a deeper relationship with the Lord. The Bible is the authority upon which every premise of the book will stand. In some areas, the Bible contradicts what society today teaches about a specific issue. It is clear, however, that true love, fullness of joy, success, courage, righteousness, peace, and rest can only come through abiding in the truth that makes men, women, and children free indeed. This, my friend, is my heart's desire for you as I share my life's work and love with you. It has taken me nearly eighty years to climb to this part of the mountain, and I want to share my view of the vista with you. When Eva and I learned that she was carrying our first child, I was age twenty-six. You might say we were at the foot of a magnificent mountain. We were eager to start the climb. Family living turned out to be steeper and more demanding than we expected. You may have already found this to be true of your own climb. Over the course of these many decades of walking up the hill with the Lord, Eva and I learned how to enjoy the journey…even when it was hardest. And that is why I am writing this book. I want you to enjoy your journey and cherish the moments you spend with the wonderful children that God has placed in your care.

1

GROWING
WITH YOUR
CHILDREN

THOUGHT STARTER

*Parental growth is as important as the physical,
mental, emotional, and spiritual growth of your children.*

MEMORY VERSE

*Train up a child in the way he should go,
and when he is old he will not depart from it.*

PROVERBS 22:6

LAUNCHING AND COMPLETING A FAMILY CAN BE COMPARED
to launching and completing a college education.

John, a senior in high school, is a brilliant student: He receives
mostly A's; is a fine athlete, a four-letter man, well liked and popular,
president of his class; from a happy Christian home; and is active in his
church youth group. We can confidently say that John has a fine background for success in college.

Even so, when he goes to college, John will, at best, be an outstanding freshman. We would not expect him to possess the knowledge,
experience, maturity, judgment, or social graces of a college senior. The

qualities of being a college senior would have to be developed over the course of four years of class attendance, study, social interaction, effort, persistence, and experiencing the results of making a range of choices each day. Becoming a successful, well-adjusted college senior is a four-year process, even for the most talented freshman. The same model holds true for anyone who is about to become a parent for the first time.

For example, some years ago I remember reading about the wedding of two young people who are very popular in our community. The article appeared in the women's section of our local newspaper. As I read about Janet and Jim's wedding, I thought about how they were bringing their own particular backgrounds into their marriage. Jim and Janet both graduated from college in the top 10 percent of their classes. Throughout their college years both of them were leaders in campus activities. Although it was obvious to everyone that these two were wonderful young people who had already accomplished much, they were still just beginners at the task of marriage. It would have been impractical to assume that as they embarked on their life together, they were equipped with the wisdom of seasoned veterans who had already raised a fine family and now looked on as their children established their own homes.

After they had been married for four years, an unexpected event came into their lives at a time when their careers, their marriage, and a pleasant social life kept them fully occupied. She was training to be a legal secretary at a prestigious law firm, and he held an enviable position with an international accounting firm where he had been chosen to participate in a four-year training program that would prepare him for a leadership position. The arrival of a baby would require a radical shift in their way of life. For the next twenty years, Janet and Jim would have an around-the-clock responsibility, regardless of whether or not they would sometimes long for the more carefree life they led before the baby was born.

RELUCTANT, INEXPERIENCED PARENTS

The Creator of the world has obviously chosen to give young, inexperienced people the responsibility for guiding the life of a baby. Often they hardly know what marriage is all about when the new baby arrives on the scene. Even with all of the parenting books and classes available today, few parents know where to begin. However, if parents cherish the moments of growing together in the grace of God as a family, they will all be blessed with greater joy than they could begin to imagine.

STAGES IN FAMILY DEVELOPMENT

Parenting, like a college education, is a process. It requires years of study, effort, persistence, and choices that all contribute to the wholesome development of the marriage.

A typical marriage will pass through several stages, including family founding, childbearing, child rearing, child launching, and the empty-nest stage. No marriage is typical of all others. Each of the stages may be longer or shorter in some marriages, and some families are in several stages at one time. Some marriages are interrupted by divorce or death. However, in marriage or family life we pass through a series of stages. Because the stages in my marriage were well defined, my wife and I were able to prepare for phases that were to come. Inevitably, some stages will be unexpected. However, those who have been rooted in a close relationship will be able to weather any storm as they cleave to their Savior and very best friend, Jesus.

My wife and I were married for two years before our childbearing stage began. Although some couples choose not to have children or are unable to have them, marriage often implies parenthood.

Developmental Stages

Although there is a direct link between abundant joy and our own personal relationship with the Lord, a parent must also be familiar with how God's creation—humans—develop and grow. For example, children are generally developmentally ready to master certain milestone tasks during certain age spans. We have provided the chart below to help you determine what developmental tasks your child is probably facing at the present time. Being familiar with these stages will help you provide the equipment and learning opportunities your child needs to develop these skills. This knowledge will also be a guidepost that will deter you from expecting your child to learn tasks before he is ready to master them. To understand their roles and tasks, parents must study each child to see at what rate he is growing in any given area and then guide the child from one developmental step to another. Being informed about human development will help you recognize and celebrate your child's accomplishments and enjoy his learning experiences.

Infancy and Early Childhood

1. Learning to walk
2. Learning to take solid foods
3. Learning to talk
4. Learning to control the elimination of body wastes
5. Learning sex differences and sexual modesty
6. Achieving physiological stability
7. Forming simple concepts of social and physical reality
8. Learning to relate oneself emotionally to parents, siblings, and other people
9. Learning to distinguish right from wrong and developing a conscience

Middle Childhood (Age 6 to 12)

1. Learning physical skills necessary for ordinary games
2. Building wholesome attitudes toward oneself
3. Learning to get along with others of own age
4. Learning to behave like boys and girls
5. Developing fundamental skills in reading, writing, and calculating
6. Developing concepts necessary for everyday living
7. Developing the conscience, morality, and a scale of values

Adolescence (Age 12 to 18)

1. Accepting one's body and a masculine or feminine role
2. Developing new relationships with others of same age
3. Becoming emotionally independent of parents and other adults
4. Achieving assurance of economic independence
5. Selecting and preparing for an occupation
6. Developing concepts and intellectual skills necessary for civic and social duty
7. Desiring and achieving socially responsible behavior
8. Preparing for marriage and family life

Early Adulthood (Age 18 to 30)

1. Selecting a mate
2. Learning to live with a marriage partner
3. Starting a family
4. Rearing children
5. Managing a home
6. Getting started in an occupation
7. Taking on civic responsibility
8. Finding a congenial social group

Middle Age (Age 30 to 55)

1. Achieving adult civic and social responsibility
2. Establishing and maintaining an economic standard of living
3. Assisting teenage children to become responsible and happy adults
4. Developing adult leisure activities
5. Falling back on the couple's role after the nest is empty
6. Accepting and adjusting to physiological changes of middle age
7. Adjusting to aging parents

Later Maturity

1. Adjusting to decreasing physical strength and health
2. Adjusting to retirement and reduced income
3. Adjusting to death of spouse
4. Becoming an active member of one's own age group
5. Establishing satisfactory living arrangements

But guess what? Your child is not the only one in your family who is learning and developing. You and your child are learning and developing at the same time…but at different levels, of course. Because you are facing developmental challenges while your children are facing other ones, we have included a list of adult developmental challenges—including the stages of marriage.

Me, an Expert?

Growing with the first child can be likened to the school teacher who is presenting a particular course for the first time. Most likely, he stays only one step ahead of his class, and until he teaches the material he has prepared, he doesn't know whether or not it will be effective. Then during the second year when he teaches the same course, the process is much easier. Because the teacher is more familiar with the material, his preparation time is greatly reduced. The material is presented much more effectively for the new class of students because the teacher has expanded from new sources after he discovered what worked with last year's students and what did not. Then, even less preparation time will be necessary if he continues to teach the course in the years to come. In time, he will have other courses to teach, sometimes new ones that require development of a new set of notes and a new teaching outline. Thus the job of the teacher is always getting bigger and more complicated.

It is the same with the parent. Dealing with the second child will be more routine than it was with the first. Things that bothered you with the first child will be "old stuff" with those who are born later. To complicate matters even more and make it even more fun, being a parent to multiple children will inherently mean that you will be guiding each child through the mastery of different developmental tasks—simultaneously.

Do not be discouraged when your child appears to require more time to master a developmental task than you expected. Children will develop at their own rates of speed. One child will master gross motor skills very easily (and be off the developmental charts for his age), but have more trouble with socialization and small motor skills (and be below what is considered typical for his age). Another child will be highly creative and easily master verbal skills, while his brother is a thinker who more easily accomplishes tasks that require fine motor skills. Enjoy your children right where they are at any given time. Yes, help the child in his areas of weakness when appropriate, but also encourage him to excel in areas that bring him great joy and excitement. Remember, God gave each of us natural talents, and parents must partner with God to help the child develop a love for and mastery of those talents. To enjoy your child to the fullest, enjoy and cherish each and every season of your lives together.

The writer of Ecclesiastes puts it this way: "To everything there is a season, a time for every purpose under heaven: a time to be born, and a time to die; a time to plant, and a time to pluck what is planted" (Ecclesiastes 3:1–2).

Isaiah asks a question of importance to parents and then answers it: "'Whom will he teach knowledge? And whom will he make to understand the message? Those just weaned from milk? Those just drawn from the breasts? For precept must be upon precept, precept upon precept, line upon line, line upon line, here a little, there a little'" (Isaiah 28:9–10).

The observant, attentive, and informed parent will be watching for his or her child's readiness to learn a new developmental task. The prepared parent will always be working toward, studying for, and praying about the challenges ahead. Changing circumstances continuously offer new challenges, new slopes to climb together. The best-qualified parent seeks help through constant reading, organized classes, government and private agencies, and the church. By putting your ideas into practice, you will gradually acquire more and more skill in the art of arranging experiences that foster wholesome, happy development. You will thereby develop understanding, and over time your conviction will deepen and widen. Parents who are unprepared will enjoy their children less than parents who fully invest in their responsibility. Prepared parents, however, will be able to recognize, facilitate, and celebrate a child's milestones. Certainly no parent has all of the answers. By the grace and design of God, children can survive many technical mistakes—if their parents are dedicated and loving. The Bible states: "Above all, love each other deeply, because love covers over a multitude of sins" (1 Peter 4:8, NIV).

Parenthood is much more than a body of techniques. Well-informed parents will thoroughly mix parenting skills with plenty of prayer, meditation on the Word of God, daily repentance, the richness of love, joy, and heaps of affection.

Remember, you are the world's greatest expert on your children.

Teachers, friends, pastors, and neighbors will come and go, but you have been called by God to be a constant, loving influence and anchor in the life of your children. Nevertheless, even though you know your own child better than anyone else, you still need to major in the study of how to help them step-by-step as they conquer one developmental milestone after another at their own rate of speed. If you are to effectively lead them in the way they ought to go, you will need to fully invest yourself in their welfare and find joy in every step.

TRAINING A BABY TO
BECOME A MATURE ADULT

In summation, successful parents will be (1) at peace within themselves and (2) happy and congenial.

Parental responsibility may be summed up in a brief Bible verse: "Train up a child in the way he should go" (Proverbs 22:6). Training or correction that produces proper conduct or action is called *discipline.*

We think of a disciplined person as one who has chosen a certain way of life and voluntarily continues in that chosen way. To "discipline" a child is to teach that child the way he or she ought to go. This includes everything you do to help the child learn.

Parents have the primary responsibility for disciplining their own children, and the school, church, other agencies, and society provide supportive roles. As parents raise their child over a twenty-year span of time, the child develops the inner strengths that enable him to take more and more responsibility for his own conduct and its consequences. Over time, the parents of the child, in turn, relinquish more and more control over his behavior and activities.

Disciplined children who have become disciplined adults will have learned the value of adhering to biblically based standards. These standards and their personal relationship with the Lord Jesus Christ will continue to shape attitudes and mold behavior. For example, disciplined children will have learned the importance of fulfilling certain lifelong commitments to home, church, school, and community. They will also have learned to face the problems of life with confidence, hope, eagerness, determination, and faith in God. The disciplined life is full of joy. These children add daily to a fund of knowledge. Primary relationships are satisfying even during times of challenge, and they face life with courage. They have a zest for living. If you have equipped your children to have a zeal for this kind of life, you have trained them well.

Parenthood is an irreversible way of life. Raising children requires a lot of energy and ingenuity. Fortunately, children generally develop in a reasonably systematic way, enabling parents to become familiar with what to expect. Parents who study the developmental tasks of family living will be better equipped to help children achieve healthy growth because they will be able to recognize the stages their children are approaching.

Training your child in the way that he should go is to teach your child to love God and keep His commandments. The tools for training are knowledge of the needs of children, knowledge of the particular child, clearly defined limits, an eagerness to personally help and supervise the child, and your own personal relationship with the Lord Jesus Christ.

The dedicated and disciplined parent will use all the skill, knowledge, and help available to interpret the needs of the children and teach them values that are based on the Word of God. Leading your children to an abundant life can be one of the greatest joys and rewards of your life.

MAKING DISCIPLES

Parenthood is the process of making disciples of your children. As Jesus walked this earth, He selected a dozen men, saying, "'Follow me'" (Matthew 4:19; see also 10:1). Before He went to the cross, He prayed: "'For I gave them the words you gave me and they accepted them. They knew with certainty that I came from you, and they believed that you sent me…. As you sent me into the world, I have sent them into the world'" (John 17:8, 18, NIV).

By studying the Gospels, it is easy to see that each disciple was an individual. Yet each one was given the same holy standard for daily living, the standard of the Lord Jesus.

In his letter to the Philippians, Paul says: "But one thing I do…I press on toward the goal to win the prize for which God has called me heavenward in Christ Jesus" (Philippians 3:13–14, NIV).

He goes on to say: "Whatever you have learned or received or heard from me, or seen in me—put it into practice. And the God of peace will be with you" (Philippians 4:9, NIV).

Thus he takes upon himself the responsibility of being a living example. Parents, too, should live as Paul did, striving for the same high calling. Fortunate is the child whose parents give her such a living example that she can safely follow in their footsteps. Fortunate is the child who has parents that can each say to her: "Whatever you have learned or received or heard from me, or seen in me—put it into practice. And the God of peace will be with you" (Philippians 4:9, NIV).

If you are following the example of the Lord Jesus Christ, you can rejoice at the thought that your children could grow up to be just like you (see Luke 6:40; 1 Corinthians 11:1). If this is not a happy thought for you, then take the steps necessary for you to become the kind of person you want your children to become. In summation, be Christlike.

The Lord Jesus and apostle Paul showed others the way they should go. Yes, they taught them, but they also showed them. Parents will teach by example *and* by words, but it is important for parents to always be aware of what it is that they are showing and teaching. Parents are living models for their children, sometimes for good and sometimes for bad. They must daily choose which it will be. As someone once said, "The best way to teach character is to have it around the house."

A student follows the teacher. As the student's guide, the teacher defines and points to the way that the student should go. In lesser or greater measure, this student is the teacher's disciple. The student learns information from the teacher and absorbs a basic philosophy on the subject. Sometimes the student will even acquire a teacher's physical mannerisms. To an even greater degree, the same is true for you and your child. Your basic job title is "nurturing and protective teacher and caregiver," and your basic job description is to lovingly help your child go in the right direction.

However, first things first: Before you can help a child go where he should go, you must know (and be absolutely convinced of) where he should go! How convinced you are can be measured by whether or not you are exhibiting that behavior in your own life.

2

RELAX
AND HAVE
FUN!

THOUGHT STARTER

God designed parenthood to be
practiced by inexperienced parents.

MEMORY VERSE

Let your father and your mother be glad,
And let her who bore you rejoice.

PROVERBS 23:25

MUCH CAN BE LEARNED FROM WHAT SOCRATES SAID IN 469 B.C.:

> If I could get to the highest place in Athens, I would lift up my voice and say, "What mean ye fellow citizens that you turn every stone to scrape wealth together and take so little care of your children, to whom you must one day relinquish it all?"

Sounds like a modern statement, doesn't it? Isn't it true that by the time you do your job, get in some recreation, and carry out your social opportunities, it becomes difficult to find time or energy to pay enough attention to your children?

If you spend a lot of time with your children, you'll learn a lot about them. You will also learn a lot about yourself. You can always count on your children to pop the bubble—to shatter the polished image you have of yourself.

I can chuckle about it now when I think of one example of how our bubble was once popped. One of our preschool children taught us a lesson we never forgot. It was when we were privileged to have a visit from our college president. It was quite an honor for a couple of young students to entertain the president of our school, and we were determined to make the most of it.

The apartment looked better than it had ever looked before. Everything was in place, polished to a high luster. Of course, we had determined to act as though it was always this way, so we carefully coached our little preschool children on what they could and couldn't say. We practically wrote them a script, but we would soon painfully pay for the sham we were creating.

Soon the president came, and we stumbled all over ourselves trying to make him comfortable. We got him to the table just fine and sat him next to our little daughter who was just learning to talk. That was a mistake. (It is interesting to note how many mistakes people can make when they are trying to put up a front.)

During the meal this little tot said to the president in her birdlike voice: "Will you please pass the salt?"

Nobody paid any attention.... We were listening to the president.

So she tried again. "Will you please pass the salt?"

This quiet, little voice was easy to ignore as we strained to hear every word the president was saying.

The third time she spoke, this little curly-haired tot single-handedly smashed all illusions about the Brandt family offspring that we had so carefully constructed. She hammered our distinguished guest on the arm and yelled: "Pass the salt or I'll knock your block off!"

I turned all shades of angry purple. The most palatable idea to me at that moment was to twist that little kid into a pretzel. Yet there was no real reason to be angry. She had simply exposed my spirit—the spirit that little Beth had seen during previous meals. Also, we should have known we were expecting too much from such a small child.

I have told this story all over the world and everyone thinks it is funny, but I sure didn't think it was funny at the time when it occurred.

Wouldn't it be great if we could enjoy our experiences as much as we enjoy talking about them later? At the time it happened, the incident seemed like a major catastrophe. Today it is a fond memory of an amusing incident.

THE SHADOW OF DEATH REVEALS LOVE

I had no idea how tender a father could feel toward his child until our little Beth developed viral pneumonia and passed under the shadow of death.

She had been crying a lot in her playpen. I accused my wife of spoiling her, but she insisted our baby was ill. We agreed to let the doctor decide. His terrible diagnosis of viral pneumonia left us weak with fear. At the time there was no known treatment. We left her alone in the hospital and went home to wait…and wait.

She got to the place where she would not respond and would not eat. I stood helplessly by the bedside of our little baby and discovered that I loved her even more than I had realized—so much so that I ached from having so much love for her. A few days earlier I had been mad at her. Now with a heart filled with love, there was nothing I would not do for her. My wife and I clung to each other, desperately praying for the life of our baby. I asked God to forgive me for my impatience and lack of concern.

Day after day I rushed to be with my daughter as soon as my classes at the college were over. Still she would not eat, so the attendants began feeding her intravenously. She continued to grow thinner and thinner. One evening I asked the nurse if I could hold my little girl, and as I held my little one in my arms, she took some milk from the bottle. She would not eat for anyone else. Only I could feed her—I who had been angry with her for crying too much; I who had actually prevented my wife from taking her to a doctor.

My insensitivity could have led to even more dire consequences, but by the grace of God, our daughter recovered. I learned the hard way that we need to know and respect our children. The Bible states it this way: "'Whoever receives one of these little children in My name receives Me; and whoever receives Me, receives not Me but Him who sent Me'" (Mark 9:37).

After that I enjoyed my child like I never had before. I still smile when I think back on the time when the same child discovered her shadow. She turned one way and it disappeared. Then it was back again. She could not run away from it. How do you explain a shadow?

When our son was a baby, I put him in a basket that was suspended between the handlebars of my bicycle. One day he fell out of the basket as we pedaled along. What a shock! When I picked him up, he had a black eye and a bruised face. I think the ordeal hurt me as much as it hurt him. Then, while I was trying to explain to my wife what had happened, I dropped him again. During moments like these we realize how tenderly we can feel toward someone.

This is the same child who came to his mother with a puzzled look on his face and said, "Mom, how come I've got pipes in my arms?" How do you explain what a bone is? Parenting is filled with moments like these. The innocence of a child brings a chuckle, a smile, and warmth in the heart of a parent whose life has been adorned with love. When moments like these are cherished, it is so easy to abide by the biblical principle: "Be kindly affectionate to one another with brotherly love, in honor giving preference to one another" (Romans 12:10).

Of course, there is another side to living with children. But even though the other side requires self-sacrifice, it will bring fullness of joy to the dedicated parent who has a thankful heart.

RELAX—YOU'VE GOT TO BE KIDDING!

I remember one of my professors telling me, "Don't make parenting so difficult. Just relax and have fun! Don't think you have to know everything in order to be a good parent."

Being a parent starts out as a dream. Doting, expectant fathers and their pregnant wives dream about the sweet, little infant all cozy in pink or blue blankets with ribbons and talcum powder. With smiles in their eyes, they turn to each other and vow, "We're going to be the best parents ever!"

Then the baby arrives. Suddenly the parents discover that "the dream" yells. And smells. And has a reversible stomach. All at 3 A.M.

Our baby cried and often was unable to be comforted. In the early months we slept little at night and very little during the day. My wife got up one night at about 3 A.M. for about the fourth time! Still asleep, she picked up the little bundle and began patting it saying, "It's okay, honey." To her surprise, she was holding a pillow she had taken out of the closet, and our baby was still in his bed screaming at the top of his lungs!

It's enough to make a grown man cry—or even worse. I can remember taking our squalling baby, shoving it toward my wife one night and saying, "You take it."

It is humbling to realize that what you thought were wonderful, parental instincts cannot always be counted on when you need them.

CHILDREN

John Wilmot once said: "Before I got married I had six theories about bringing up children; now I have six children, and no theories."

Imagine a big man letting a tiny baby make him angry! Yet it happens all the time.

Children's antics will stir up what is in your heart. If there is anger, impatience, selfishness, meanness, malice, cruelty, or partiality in your heart, children will bring it out for display. Although it is not often considered to be a benefit of family life, children will help you stay up-to-date on your spiritual condition.

CONFIDENT EXPECTATION

During my graduate work at Cornell University, the faculty experimented with different methods of helping children and parents. These were cleverly done. One well-thought-out series involved mothers who could not control their children. The incidents were recorded on film and then shown to various classes.

I will never forget the one about the mother who could not feed her son applesauce. Every time she tried, the boy shoved the spoon away. This was the cue for the mother to turn to the researcher and shrug.

"See? He just won't eat it."

The researcher told her to try again, which she did—unsuccessfully. Finally the mother gave up.

"This happens all the time," the mother said.

Then one of the teachers tried it. Although her mannerism was both gentle and firm, it was obvious that she was determined to feed that child applesauce. At first the child shoved the spoonful of applesauce aside when he saw it coming toward his mouth, but the teacher was undaunted by the child's resistance. Without hesitation she brought the spoon back up and right into the child's mouth.

Gulp! One spoonful of applesauce down the hatch. The child was surprised and the mother even more so.

The teacher did it again. This time the child was ready and pushed the spoon away, but the teacher again steadily returned the spoon back and around the little fist. Once more, the applesauce popped into the child's mouth. Another surprised gulp. Now the child had two spoonfuls of applesauce in his stomach.

A third thrust with the spoon again succeeded. The fourth thrust went in without any resistance from the child at all.

Soon the child was enjoying the applesauce. In no time at all, the teacher had emptied the entire dish of applesauce—one spoonful at a time—into the child's now willing mouth.

WHY THE DIFFERENCE?

There were two reasons for the women's differing results. First, a handy tool called *confident expectation.*

This assumes that what is being required is in the best interest of the child. The caregiver, who believes this, will have enough conviction to see the action through. In the illustration above, the teacher's determination reflected her resolve that helping the child eat the applesauce was in the toddler's best interest.

Second, as was exhibited in the case of the teacher in the study, any caregiver's manner will need to be friendly, gentle, and firm.

To help the mother understand the difference in the two approaches, the teacher explained what had led to the mother's inability to overcome the child's resistance. Because the mother had been taking her cues from that little child, she had expected to fail. A little bit of resistance (which is normal in human beings) from the small child was enough to frustrate a grown woman.

In the next few sessions the mother watched the teacher successfully feed bowl after bowl of applesauce to the child. It is important to note one other thing that was obvious in all the sessions. The teacher was not forcing the applesauce into the child's mouth just to prove a point. Because her manner was friendly, gentle, and firm, it was obvious that she wanted to help the child eat something that was healthful.

The teacher taught the mother that although resistance is to be expected from children, it can be overcome with gentle, well-founded pressure—pressure that is based on confident expectation.

After she had observed the teacher for a few days, the mother was urged to try again. The child took one look at the setup—the bowl of applesauce…the spoon…the mother. It all came back to him. He knew his role in this drama: Resist.

However, he was up against a mother who was now informed and different. This time the mother was dedicated to success. She was convinced she was assisting her child.

She took a spoonful of applesauce and directed it toward the child. *Aha!* The child's thinking was mirrored on his face as he batted the spoon away.

But the mother immediately brought the spoon back toward him. With a gleam in his eye, he shoved it aside again. This time she brought it back more quickly than he expected and before he knew what had happened, the spoonful of applesauce disappeared into his pouting mouth.

Gulp. The child could not believe his taste buds. The surprised look on his face was truly a sight to see.

The mother's expression was incredible. You would have thought she had just inherited a million dollars. Her face wore a million-dollar glow of triumph. She was victorious! She had placed a spoonful of applesauce into her child's mouth. Soon, the child sensed the difference too, and he responded to his mother's inviting, gentle, and firm manner. Before the bowl was empty, the scene had changed to a mother feeding applesauce to a willing and cooperative child.

Remember that phrase: *confident expectation.* If you are to give your children the guidance they need, you must be convinced that your efforts will benefit them.

ME, AN AUTHORITY?

Success, however, implies that you have received wisdom from God and you know your child well. James 1:5–6 is very clear about what a Christian is to do if he lacks wisdom:

> If any of you lacks wisdom, let him ask of God, who gives to
> all liberally and without reproach, and it will be given to him.
> But let him ask in faith, with no doubting, for he who doubts
> is like a wave of the sea driven and tossed by the wind.

So, if you lack wisdom, ask God to give it to you and have faith that you will receive it. As for knowing your children, you can be the world's greatest authority on the subject of your children—if you pay attention to them. And, of course, that's the catch. To become an authority on your children, you must work at it. You must talk with them, listen to them, play with them, read to them, pray with them, work with them, and spend time with them. Your role is imperative. In fact, parents play the most strategic role in society.

As for my wife and me, you might say that our days of giving full-time care to our children have come and gone because we have raised all of our children to the point where they are now living out on their own. Actually, I like this empty-nest stage the best. Yes, we enjoyed our time with our kids immensely, but I am glad the suspense is over. I say this because the very nature of being a parent is suspenseful. I believe every parent wonders, *How will my children turn out?*

My wife and I used these principles from the time when our children were quite small. These principles made those years of parenthood a pleasant time. They worked for us—and for thousands of parents who have counseled with me—and I am fully confident that they will work for you.

In fact, the principles I will be sharing with you in this book have been so effective for other families over a period of forty years that parents have been coming to me to tell me how much they have been helped by them. I have taught these principles at major conferences and seminars around the world, and they have brought simplicity to the parenting process and have helped parents relax and enjoy their children.

Parenthood should be enjoyable, even during those years we fear the most. The teenage years, for example, can be the greatest time of all.

Parenthood is not difficult, but it is demanding. It takes time, some deep convictions, your own good example, knowledge of your kids, following the teachings of the Bible, and a loving spirit. Never forget that the One who knows your children's needs better than you is Jesus Christ. He knows things you do not know, and when you have a close relationship with Him, you will know the truth about your children (see Jeremiah 33:3; John 8:31–32).

Parents are strategic, important people who are involved in one of the greatest adventures of life. Never let go of the dream of being the best parent ever.

You can expect success—and also learn from your children. Expect to grow, to change, and to improve.

3

I'M NOT HAVING FUN YET!

THOUGHT STARTER

*Considering others better than yourself
is a good start to good parenting.*

MEMORY VERSE

*Let each of you look out not only for his own interests,
but also for the interests of others.*

PHILIPPIANS 2:4

LET'S HAVE FUN. WONDERFUL INGREDIENTS FOR HAVING fun include expecting success and developing meaningful relationships while you learn, develop, and grow as you "parent."

These ingredients describe what every parent really wants. Indeed, these concepts must be central to your adventure into enjoyable parenthood. For a moment though, let's digress. Let's look at some parents who are not having fun.

Why get into the negative? Simple. Because *most* parents are not having much fun.

Perry Manning's folks fought with each other nearly every day over something Perry did or wanted to do. So Perry figured it was just another battle of words when his parents squared off over the issue of his car.

"That boy is a menace on the road," he heard his mother say.

"He'll mature," replied his dad.

"But half the time we don't know where he is," his mother cut in.

"Well, you can't fence in a seventeen-year-old," his dad said.

Then Perry heard them pick up their long-standing quarrel over what Christian training is and what it is not. He knew they would reach a stalemate again, and as usual, he would just go on doing what he wanted to do while they continued to postpone making a decision about what he should and should not do.

As they continued their indecisive haggling over his behavior, Perry collected a few traffic tickets and found a buddy to bump out fenders. After his graduation he was out almost every night, and he began dating a girl with questionable reputation.

"Oh, don't worry about Perry and that girl," his dad said to Perry's mother. "I went with five girls before I met you. I'll put a stop to this nonsense."

His response to the situation was to quickly plan a family trip to Yellowstone. Perry rode with his parents to the national park, but the day he turned eighteen he caught a bus headed for home.

The Mannings returned home, too—and then headed straight to the Christian Counseling Clinic to see what they could do about their son.

"There's nothing you can do," I said to the two tearful parents, "except pray to God that your boy will come to his senses."

They had long ago relinquished control of their son when they failed to agree on how to raise him. The spirit of conflict between mother and father had prevented them from exercising any parental judgment. How different things would have been had they practiced the following scriptural teaching:

> Now I plead with you, brethren, by the name of our Lord Jesus Christ, that you all speak the same thing, and that there be no divisions among you, but that you be perfectly joined together in the same mind and in the same judgment.
>
> 1 CORINTHIANS 1:10

Somehow they could not find an answer to Perry's searching question the day he left them. Perry asked, "If what I'm doing at eighteen is so terrible, why wasn't it bad enough to stop me at seventeen?"

The Bible says to "train up a child in the way he should go, and when he is old he will not depart from it" (Proverbs 22:6). The Bible further states, "Be kindly affectionate to one another with brotherly love, in honor giving preference to one another" (Romans 12:10).

If these truths are applied to parenthood, the way a child should go becomes a matter of parental decision, with a foundation of affection that is first exhibited between the parents and then toward the children. Parents quickly discover that children tend to go their own way, just as they themselves do.

As I indicated in the last chapter, the demands of parenthood expose the soul. They reveal the quality of the marriage partnership and the character of each parent.

I have seen a common pattern among parents I have counseled who have been having difficulty with their children. I have found that the parents generally hold differing opinions about what the limits should be, how to deal with the child's resistance, or the degree to which the child should be supervised. In summation, the root of the problem is usually in the parent-to-parent relationship and not in the parent-to-child relationship.

When parents are divided by some form of selfishness, each parent must take responsibility for the conflict, repent of selfishness and irritability, and receive forgiveness from God. Each may have a change of heart. The marriage relationship can then be restored. In a spirit of kindly affection toward each other, the parents can resolve the issues over establishing limits, patterns for supervising the child, and methods of dealing with the child's resistance. Having a changed heart will also enable the parent to deal with the child firmly—but without malice.

To some this may seem too simplistic. But if sin is the problem, Matthew 1:21 states that "JESUS...He will save His people from their sins." This is the express purpose of why Jesus came. Paul stated in 2 Corinthians 11:3, "But I fear, lest somehow, as the serpent deceived Eve by his craftiness, so your minds may be corrupted from the simplicity that is in Christ."

Many people try to solve a sin problem by using human means to resolve the issue. But if sin is the problem, no human remedy is available. If sin is the problem, Christ is the cure. He came preaching that we should repent, for the kingdom of heaven is at hand. When two people have a clean heart, the marriage relationship can be restored.

The issue is simple: Sin will corrupt a marriage. The answer is simple: Jesus came to save us from our sin. Remember, though, that simple does not necessarily imply *easy.*

In instances where the parents are divorced, the father and mother must still present a united front. Even if the marriage is not restored, the parents should work toward being in agreement about setting consistent limits for the children regardless of which household the child is staying at during a given period of time.

WHEN YOUR DREAM DOES NOT
MATCH YOUR CIRCUMSTANCES

Sensible couples—or single parents—start out planning for their family to be the best ever, but then discover that the work has just begun. In all my years of counseling, I have never had one parent or set of parents come to me and say, "Well, here we are, Dr. Brandt. We are bursting with mutual admiration because we've succeeded at reaching our goal. Our objective was to create an intolerable situation for all of us. Now we've done it: We have created the perfect mess we strived so hard for. We can't stand each other."

Of course, people do not set such goals. Well then, why is this marital upheaval in our society happening? Many good people start marriage with the highest of hopes and end up hopelessly at odds. The idea of personal freedom becomes an obsession and marriage and parenthood become a nightmare with no apparent solution. But Jesus approached this attitude in the Bible by saying: "'If anyone desires to come after Me, let him deny himself'" (Luke 9:23).

The life of a parent is full of choices about how each will respond to the other parent and how he or she will respond to their children. Their attitudes and actions will be a reflection of the strength of their relationship with God. If they have a close relationship with Him, their responses will be much more Christlike and will grow more so each day. On the other hand, their responses will be empty and selfish if they have been self-centered instead of God-centered.

Avoiding conflict with the child is not the appropriate basis for parents to make decisions about their child. Avoiding a clash of opinions with the child is usually a form of taking the easy way out. After all, it is important to give our children the freedom to make their own decisions, isn't it? As an example, let's consider a mother who goes into her child's room in the morning and rouses her. The following dialogue ensues:

Mother: Well, shall we get up today?

Child: No. (Child closes her eyes and burrows back down under the covers.)

Mother: You have to get up to put your dress on. You do want to get dressed, don't you?

Child: No. (Child snuggles down tighter than ever, pulling a pillow over her head.)

Mother: You can eat breakfast after you put your dress on. You'd like to do that, wouldn't you?

Child: (A sound emerges from underneath the pillow that could be translated only as another "no" statement.)

Mother: After breakfast you can watch TV. You'd like that, wouldn't you?

Child: (No answer at all now.)

And so it goes. Every morning this mother goes through the same twenty-minute, nerve-wracking ritual as she cajoles her child into getting up for another day. The mother here takes this approach because she wants to avoid conflict. When we assess this mother-daughter dialogue, we can see how the mother allowed her daughter room to say "no" when there really was no room for a "no" answer. Of course, the child does not want to get up, so don't ask her if that is what she wants to do. Allowing the child to think she has a choice when she really does not have one is a strong invitation for the child to misunderstand what you are saying and then resist what you initially intended for her to do.

Other questions that give mixed messages include: Shall we make our bed and pick up our room? Shall we eat breakfast? Shall we drink our milk? Shall we go to school? Aren't you staying out too late? Aren't you running with the wrong crowd?

Of course, resistance will occur no matter how the parent phrases the request—if the parent continues to leave the door open for the child to choose to respond in unacceptable ways.

THE NIGHTMARE

One mother described to me a completely fruitless dialogue that had become an everyday occurrence at home with her thirteen-year-old son.

Mother: It's time to take out the garbage.

Son: (No response.)

Mother: (Irritated.) I said it's time to take out the garbage!

Son: All right…all right.

Mother: (Angry and losing control.) Well, don't just stand there! I said: Take out the garbage!

Finally the son stirs and goes through the evening ritual of taking out the garbage. As usual, he leaves one sack. Then he sits down again.

Mother: (Now screaming.) You stupid, rebellious kid! Get the rest of that garbage and take it out…and don't try to tell me you didn't see…

It is easy to see why this mother felt so defeated when she came to my office.

"I just hate myself. I'm turning into a mess. I'm just nothing but a screaming, old nag of a mother," she complained.

Remember what I mentioned earlier: Children's antics will stir up what is in your heart.

The opportunity for self-discovery lasts for at least twenty years. For some parents, this is good news. For most, this is a scary thought. Why? Because we may not like what we see. At the office we can look good most of the time. At our club meetings we can appear pretty much in control. But we cannot pretend twenty-four hours a day—in our own home. By its very nature, parenthood will not allow us to hide the worst side of ourselves. And worse yet, we certainly would rather not see our faults mirrored in our children's lives. Again, the answer is repentance.

TRAINING BY EXAMPLE

Our example can have dire effects on our children. This was true for a woman named Mrs. Greene when she had the rude awakening of seeing herself in her teenage daughter. By observing her mother over the years, Laurie had learned Mrs. Greene's means of control well. When Mrs. Greene wanted to move and her husband did not, she managed to find so much to criticize about the house that the family ended up moving.

Then after the family moved into their new home, Mr. Greene thought they could not afford new carpeting, but his wife proved they could. Mrs. Greene also talked her husband into installing an extra phone line for their daughter, Laurie. Then, when Mrs. Greene wanted to exchange a long-planned camping trip for a trip to the world's fair, she pouted until everyone came around to her view.

Mrs. Greene did not appear to be a demanding woman. Appearances aside, though, with full consciousness of her methods, she imposed her will on others, either subtly or directly.

Her teenage daughter, Laurie, went her own way, ignoring her father and working around her mother's dominance. Her wants were seldom out of line, so there were few conflicts—until Ray came along.

"Raymond isn't good enough for you," Mrs. Greene proclaimed. (Not a good opening for the discussion.)

"Why do you say that?"

"He's not a Christian," her mother replied. "And he'll never hold down a decent job." (Not a good continuing remark.)

"But we love each other," insisted Laurie.

Her persuasion ineffective, Mrs. Greene flatly told Laurie that she was not to see Ray anymore.

"But I will! I will!" screamed Laurie.

Mrs. Greene brought to bear every device she had ever used to control a situation. She cried; she threatened; she went to bed with headaches; she tried shaming Laurie; and she told Ray she did not approve of him. But Laurie refused to budge.

Mrs. Greene asked her husband for help. But long ago he had learned to be neutral. Then Mrs. Greene came to our clinic, asking us to make Laurie see the error of her way.

After we heard the story, we told Mrs. Greene, "You seem to have forgotten the truth of God's Word, which says: 'Do not be deceived, God is not mocked; for whatever a man sows, that he will also reap.'

"You have trained your daughter well by your example of getting what you want, in any way that it takes to get it. When Laurie stubbornly resists, you are seeing yourself in your own daughter. Because you have molded her in your own image, only God can break the mold. You will just have to wait to see if He does this in spite of the foundation that has already been laid."

We also explained to Mrs. Greene that parenting through intimidation and manipulation is not an appropriate means of guiding a child. By this time, Laurie should have known that it was not a good choice for her to date a man who was not a Christian.

Rather than trying to manipulate her daughter, Mrs. Greene could have lovingly taken her daughter to the Word of God and shown her how this could not have been the will of God for her to be unequally yoked together with an unbeliever. However, this groundwork needed to have been laid long ago.

Teen years do not sneak up on a parent. It takes the child thirteen years to become a teenager. Thirteen years is a long time, and the relationship established between parents and children in the earlier years will determine whether or not the teen is prepared to make choices that are based on godly examples and principles.

God will have touched the heart of parents many times to pray for their children in those thirteen years. Sadly, many parents do not take the time to pray for their children until the children are adults.

Prayerlessness on the part of parents will leave its mark.

Parents who have prayerfully worked together as a team will have established a foundation of good communication among themselves and with their child. God will be at the center of their family if He is at the center of the life of each parent.

Some Scriptures that are debated by parents and sociologists today are: "Correct your son, and he will give you rest; yes, he will give delight to your soul" (Proverbs 29:17), and "The rod and rebuke give wisdom, but a child left to himself brings shame to his mother" (Proverbs 29:15).

By the time a child reaches the teen years, his parents will have had ample time to test these admonitions and to develop some firm convictions about the need to train, correct, and supervise. On the other hand, if parents remain divided on these issues, a teen's growing resistance to limits will bring these uncertainties and divisions to light.

The family dynamics described earlier show how teenagers will not respect parents who lack conviction or are unable to agree on decisions related to the child. The good news is that all hope is not lost when parents do not find resolve until the child reaches the teen years. God can answer prayers and intervene, and it is possible for parents to regain the respect and cooperation of their children if they begin to demonstrate their conviction to abide by what they have determined is best for each child.

FAMILY RESCUE NEEDED!

A swimming teacher was describing how to properly rescue a drowning person. As I listened, I was fascinated by the little-known precautionary step called *the quick reverse*.

> "The quick reverse," said the teacher, "is used when the rescuer comes close to the victim. This is the moment of greatest potential danger because a drowning victim is desperate and

irrational. If he can, he will grab the lifeguard and immobilize or even drown him.

"A good quick reverse stops the rescuer's momentum before he gets hopelessly and fatally trapped. It also moves the lifesaver out of the victim's reach, but the lifesaver doesn't abandon the victim. The quick reverse enables the rescuer to calmly study the victim, approach him safely, take charge, and tow him to safety.

"A knowledgeable rescuer does not panic, regardless of the victim's behavior. He takes command, acts decisively (even if the victim struggles against him), and helps the victim reach a common goal: safety.

"But a good lifesaver does not dive in every time he sees someone struggling. He does not tamper with the child who is just learning how to swim and struggling along the side of the pool. It is important for that child to be allowed to work on the problem himself.

"A good lifesaver gets involved only when there's trouble brewing. He has to be calm, happy, cooperative, able, under control, and trained. If he is not, a crisis situation will cause him to panic. He might run away from it, completely deserting the pool he has agreed to guard. He might also swim out and realize he is incapable of rescue and let the victim sink. Or he might swim right into the arms of danger, get grabbed by the victim, and end up part of a double drowning."

To some of us, the teacher's speech may seem highly technical. Notice, though, how it parallels parenthood. Just like the swimmers at a pool, children in a family situation are looking for fun in life, pleasure, fellowship, and good health.

Yet sometimes they get into trouble. Just like the swimmer who gets in trouble, the child does not plan to drown. He simply lacks knowledge. Maybe he is unprepared, lacks ability or training, ignores obvious dangers, or disobeys the rules.

Regardless, when a child is drowning in life's problems, he needs to be rescued. He needs a capable "lifesaver" to come after him and tow him to safety. He needs a parent who is ready to move in at the first sign of danger.

Yet many children are not rescued. Tragically, their parents are in no position to help because the parents themselves are either out of control, sinking, or have no plan.

Unequipped parents are in a position of weakness and are trapped in a never-ending series of crises. They seem unable to change their direction and have no idea of any alternatives. Oftentimes, they see no other alternative…because they are afraid that if they don't quickly jump ship themselves, they will drown too.

Instead, their lives need a quick reverse.

SHORT-LIVED VOW

Serious parents do not wake up in the morning planning to make their child's life miserable. No parent vows each morning: "Today I'm going to be grumpy, crabby, and impossible."

Can you imagine approaching parenthood with this attitude? Imagine you are in a maternity waiting room with an expectant father. Suddenly the father-to-be looks up at the ceiling and says with a strong tinge of iron-willed determination, "Boy, oh boy, this baby is going to regret having me as a father. I'm going to draw on all the ingenuity and creativity possible to make this little tike's life utterly miserable."

No. It does not work that way. When the alarm goes off, it is just the opposite. "Today will be different," the mother vows. "It will be a great day. No screaming, no impatient orders, no arguing."

As Mom is making her vow, a situation is developing that will easily crush that well-meaning vow. In the hall outside the bathroom, her son is beating on the door. "Hey, who's in there? You've been tying up the bathroom for half an hour. Do you think you're the only one who has to go to school?"

"Oh, buzz off!" comes the answer from big sister. "If you want to use the bathroom, why don't you go down in the basement and use the bathroom down there?"

"Why should I always have to be the one who uses the basement bathroom? Come on now, open up. Now! Or I'll tell Mom!" This threat is accompanied by a drumroll on the door.

Just then Mother comes on the scene. She finds herself in the middle of a battle between a child who wants to use the bathroom and another who is probably dawdling.

It does not take long for the mother to get into the controversy. Several screams, protests, and mutterings later, she has settled the controversy, but now she is irritated and upset. Yet only minutes before she had vowed that this would be a perfect day.

DAD GETS INVOLVED TOO

Often the same happens for the well-intentioned dad. Just before he pulls into the driveway as he comes home from work, he vows, "Tonight I'm not going to be a grouch. Tonight I'm going to have fun with the family."

Suddenly, in spite of his many lectures, he finds that his pathway to the garage is blocked by two bicycles parked in the driveway.

He parks the car halfway in the driveway and halfway in the street. Leaving the engine running, he abruptly gets out of the car and runs toward the house. Dad is hardly in the front door of the house before he is after everyone in sight. "How many times do I have to tell you guys? Get those bicycles out of the driveway! How am I going to get my car in the garage if I can't even get to it?"

Dad is out of control—just making noise without getting any facts. He continues yelling, turning now on his wife. Without one loving gesture or question, he lays her out too. "I thought I made it clear that bicycles should not be parked in the driveway." And the fight is on....

The mom at breakfast...the father coming home from work—both found themselves in a crisis situation. They blew the rescue, didn't they? They are missing the mark of having an enjoyable life.

When we have missed the mark, we all look for the cause of the awful feelings and behavior we display around the people we love most.

You may be wondering, *What mark?*

You may be surprised by the fact that "the mark" is easily defined. In fact, everyone I have ever counseled has expressed the same basic longings, the same goals—or mark. Everyone is striving to

1. enjoy life every day;
2. obtain peace that keeps their thoughts quiet and their hearts at rest;
3. increase in love toward one another;
4. be unselfish and considerate.

Would you be surprised if I told you that this is not an impossible dream? These attributes can characterize your life. They do not represent some distant, unreachable oasis.

Are you interested?

THE BEGINNING OF THE "FAMILY CURE"

Now let's examine the problem, the cause, and the cure for unhappiness.

But first—a warning!

I have watched many people explode with rage when I tried to explain the reasons for this behavior. I mention this only to warn you ahead of time that my answer comes from a source you may have rejected—God's Word, the Bible.

"Don't give me that Bible stuff!" shouted one of my clients. "I've had that crammed down my throat ever since I was a kid."

Yet, after listening and obeying what God said in His Word, this same man saw his life turned around. He followed steps that have meant new life and happy parenthood for many, many richly blessed people.

For example, did you know that what you want for yourself (joy, peace, love, unselfishness, kindness) is described in the Bible as God's will for you?

Are you still with me?

Let's start with the first questions....Why do I act the way I sometimes do? Why do I miss the mark?

Actually, the Bible describes this problematic condition like this: "For the good that I will to do, I do not do; but the evil I will not to do, that I practice" (Romans 7:19).

Yes, everyone misses the mark. Maybe you are one of the many who vowed that your marriage would be the greatest. Now you would settle for getting through breakfast without a squabble. And you do not seem to be able to control yourself.

What's the cause? A mysterious stranger within you will not behave the way you intend to behave. The Bible says the cause is sin: "Now if I do what I will not to do, it is no longer I who do it, but sin that dwells in me" (Romans 7:20).

Did I use the wrong word? It is an ugly word in a sense. Before you dismiss it, though, think for a minute. If I had used the word *virus* or *cancer,* you would listen.

Even though you may not like the word *sin,* it is an accurate description of the cause of the problems we have been addressing. However, I encourage you not to get hung up on the word and miss some very important truths such as this one: "'There is none who does good, no, not one'" (Romans 3:12).

"What do you mean: I've never done any good? I've done a lot of good in my life," you say.

Yes indeed, you have had many happy moments with your family and been generous to other people. But that is not the basis of the problem we are addressing here. Right now we are taking a look at fits of temper, deeply buried resentment, or selfishness.

It is important to note here that other people's behaviors do not excuse our own sin. Along with this, we all are sunk if our own peace of mind is dependent upon someone else's choices, behavior, or moods. Take heart, my friend; we are all in the same boat. We all need to have our lives and wills buried with Christ. Without Him, we will find ourselves powerless to exude joy, peace, and gentleness in the face of disagreements, bathroom fights, bicycles in the driveway, smelly diapers, or squalling babies.

THE JOY MACHINE IS MISSING

Do not be dismayed. God's Word describes and proclaims our need for the Savior and for a personal and intimate relationship with Him. You are not alone. We were not designed to live a righteous and bountiful life without Him. We all need Him at the center of our lives and hearts. Marriage and parenthood more clearly reveal our desperate need for Him.

Now that you know that family problems are rooted in sin, you can be comforted by the fact that Jesus is a wonderful physician who will perform surgery on those areas where you need His touch. Trying to wish the problems away—or ignoring them—will not change anything. God's will is for you to have an abundant life, and through Him you may have all He has to give you.

THE CURE

God has a plan to save you from yourself, from your sins. You have everything to gain and nothing to lose from Him. The Bible says that God will do for you what you cannot do for yourself: He will help you love others (see 1 Thessalonians 3:12).

This is what you are yearning for. Let God give you what He has promised. Your reactions toward your family will change when you have hidden yourself in Him, allowed Him to heal you, and prayed for Him to reveal to you the deep roots of sin that you cannot see by yourself.

The Bible describes the problem and its cause, but also spells out a solution: "O wretched man that I am! Who will deliver me from this body of death? I thank God—through Jesus Christ our Lord!" (Romans 7:24–25).

This is a name that sometimes makes people see red—Jesus Christ. People sometimes mistakenly associate Him with unreasonable demands, punishment, or guilt. But let Him speak for Himself. "'For God did not send His Son into the world to condemn the world, but that the world through Him might be saved'" (John 3:17).

Saved from what? Our nastiness, of course. Our sins. A sinner is like a traffic violator who has broken a traffic law. Nothing can change the fact that he is a violator. We have all experienced the sense of relief that comes when we get through a twenty-mph traffic zone after we have been speeding at forty.

This same kind of tension comes when we have missed a mark of our own. We are vaguely aware of violating something, but what do we do about it? The answer to our problems and the deepest desires of our hearts can only be found in Jesus Christ. It is said of Him: "'You shall call His name JESUS, for He will save His people from their sins'" (Matthew 1:21).

Jesus said: "'I am the way, the truth, and the life. No one comes to the Father except through Me'" (John 14:6). He stands at the door and knocks. If we hear His voice and open the door, He will come in and fellowship with us (see Revelation 3:20).

So how, then, do we approach God?

1. We start by recognizing that missing the mark is sin. We agree with God that our sins have separated us from Him.
2. Next, faith is required. The only one way to approach God is to choose to believe in Him and act on that belief.
3. We must trust Jesus as our own personal Savior.
4. We must confess our sins: It's like a man going forty in a twenty-mph zone and then taking his foot off the accelerator and asking God for His forgiveness. He agrees with the speed-limit sign that indicates he is violating a rule. This is what confession is. We admit we were wrong. And when we confess our sins, "He is faithful and just to forgive us our sins and to cleanse us from all unrighteousness" (1 John 1:9).
5. We must repent of our sins. When we repent, we have changed our minds; we have determined that we will no longer be a violator, and we have a plan and resolve to change.

You can approach God right now through prayer (prayer is talking with God). Here is a sample prayer:

Lord Jesus, I need You. I open the door of my life and receive You as my Savior and Lord. Thank You for forgiving my sins. Take control of my life. Make me the kind of person You want me to be.

When you follow this plan of salvation, Jesus will forgive you and cleanse your life of sin. Habits that once controlled you will lose their grip. As your relationship with Him grows as you spend time in prayer and in His Word, your mind will be renewed in Him and your character and nature will become increasingly more like His. The more time you spend with Him, the more you will become like Him.

Why settle for anything less? God can change your reactions to life. He can give you the resources you need to have a truly abundant life. This is the quick reverse. This is the first step to enjoyable parenthood. As you spend time with Him, He will reveal deep areas of sin in your heart and life that you need to confess and turn from. When this happens or when you see you have not responded in a way that He would respond, repeat steps 4 and 5—and then praise Him for His wonderful mercy, grace, and love.

I encourage you to use the charts on the next two pages like a mirror and as an inspiration to be more like Him. On the left-hand side are the qualities that God will help you develop. On the right-hand side is a list of sins that He will help you overcome. I am also including this chart in order to more clearly establish that family problems are often rooted in the parents' sins.

Note: The chart is based on Mark 7:21–23, Romans 1:28–31, Galatians 5:19–21, Ephesians 4:25–31, and 2 Timothy 3:1–5.

Spirit-Controlled Living versus Sin-Controlled Living

Spirit-Filled Mind	Sins of the Mind
• Forgiveness	• Unforgiveness
• Hope	• Evil thoughts
• Appreciation	• Covetousness
• Willingness	• Greed
• Impartiality	• Lust
• Self-control	• Arrogance
• Merciful	• Senseless
• Humility	• Despiteful
• Thankfulness	• Pride
• Confidence	• Ingratitude
• Wisdom	• Selfish ambition
• Faithful	• Deceitfulness
• Gratitude	• Heartless
	• Faithless
	• High and mighty

Spirit-Filled Emotions	Sinful Emotions
• Love	• Hatred
• Peace	• Rebellion
• Gentle spirit	• Bitterness
• Gladness	• Envy
• Joy	• Bad temper
• Long-suffering	• Anger
• Kindly spirit	• Unloving
• Patience	• Bad attitude
• Compassionate	• Jealousy
	• Malice
	• Rage

Spirit-Controlled Living versus Sin-Controlled Living

Spirit-Filled Mouth	Sins of the Mouth
• Truthfulness	• Lying
• Thankfulness	• Complaining
• Gentle answer	• Yelling
• Encouraging	• Boasting
• Tactful praise	• Gossip
• Timeliness	• Slandering
• Soothing	• Disputing
• Pleasant words	• Backbiting
	• Quarrelsome
	• Blasphemy

Spirit-Filled Behavior	Sinful Behavior
• Kindness	• Fornication
• Righteousness	• Adultery
• Obedience	• Drunkenness
• Goodness	• Murder
• Courage	• Insulting
• Endurance	• Ruthless
• Considerate	• Divisive
• Gentleness	• Disobedience to parents
• Self-control	• Brutality
• Cooperation	• No self-control
• Sincerity	• Stealing
• Servant	• Violence
• Submissive	• Brawling
• Impartial	• Favoritism

QUICK REVERSE "BACKLASH"

If you have decided you need a quick reverse in your life and have determined to have a permanent relationship with Jesus Christ, your family may be surprised, and possibly confused, by the sudden reverse. Do not be discouraged by this.

A business friend of mine recently took the same step you have just taken. Noticing a difference in his life, his wife asked him what had happened. When he said he had asked Jesus Christ to take charge of his life, she shook her head and muttered, "Religion, eh? You'll get over it. It was the American Legion last year...the Boy Scouts the year before.... It's just another one of your little excursions."

This is a common reaction, but you are not alone. God will be working on behalf of your family to bring them to His side if they are not already there. Do not try to overwhelm and alienate them with your new approach to life. Allow time for your expressions of the love of Christ to draw your loved ones to a personal relationship and abundant life with Him.

4

PARTNERS, NOT OPPONENTS!

THOUGHT STARTER

Husband and wife can choose to be partners or opponents, but opponents cannot be effective parents.

MEMORY VERSE

Submitting to one another in the fear of God.

EPHESIANS 5:21

DOESN'T THE WORD *PARTNERS* HAVE A PLEASANT RING TO IT? It reminds me of some other nice words: harmony...together...cooperation...agreement...appreciation...respect...success.

Of course, I fully recognize that the readers of this book may be single parents or divorced parents who have been remarried. Regardless of your marital status, however, I encourage you to read these next two chapters that focus on marriage. Why? Because you will need to teach your children about the components of a healthy marriage. Single parents will not necessarily have a model of marriage for their children to see on a daily basis, so some of the components of this model will need to be taught more than caught. This information will also help divorced and remarried parents see the need for working well with the other parent even if the two parents are living in separate households.

Children of divorced parents will try to play one parent against the other—much in the same way children of parents who are still married do. Divorced parents who present a united front when it comes to the care of the children will provide the needed consistency and a sense of safety and security for everyone concerned. Regardless of their own marital status, parents will be preparing their boys to be husbands and fathers, and preparing their girls to be wives and mothers.

FORMING THE FOUNDATION
FOR A HEALTHY MARRIAGE

Any partnership is entered into with high hopes. Partners hope to combine their resources, talents, and abilities in their efforts to achieve satisfaction and success. Of course, partnerships are generally established between people who have confidence in the other person and who are fairly certain that the partnership will be mutually beneficial.

A business partnership is one example. For the sake of illustration we will say that four men and women agree to form a partnership to build some apartment houses. Between them, they must do the following:

1. Borrow the needed money
2. Develop a set of building plans
3. Acquire the land
4. Construct the building
5. Manage the building
6. Manage the income

This is not a complete list, but it shows that a partnership requires resources, talent, cooperation, and agreement. Assuming the partners are honest people of goodwill, the project should give them a great deal of satisfaction and a sense of success. A good partnership that coincides with the ways of God will have the following attributes listed in Philippians 2:2–3 "Fulfill my joy by being like-minded, having the same love, being of one accord, of one mind. Let nothing be done through selfish ambition or conceit, but in lowliness of mind let each esteem others better than himself."

Although the formation of a partnership is a relatively simple matter, achieving the objectives for which it was formed is not so simple. Keeping God at the center of any partnership takes a lot of hard work, self-denial, and reliance upon God.

PARENTHOOD IS A PARTNERSHIP

Parents are not without purpose when they combine their love, personal relationships with the Lord, developing talents, and blessings. Their purpose is to raise mature, happy, faithful adults who exhibit the nature and characteristics of Christ in their daily lives. Again, regardless of your marital status, you will need to communicate this information to your children in order to help them develop and grow in their own future relationships. Remember that the Bible sums up the parents' objective like this: "Train up a child in the way he should go, and when he is old he will not depart from it" (Proverbs 22:6).

Although fulfilling this objective is a formidable task, it is actually a daily part of a parent's walk with the Lord. Parents are not only partnering with each other, but also partnering with the Lord as He reveals His wisdom and love, and provides the needed grace for each and every day. The parents who give their best efforts will have Jesus at the center of their own lives, and His ways will be the guidepost for daily living, facing life's challenges, and lovingly remaining committed to one another through whatever hardships may come.

THE ONE BIG HANG-UP

During my years as a counselor, I have heard thousands of sad stories about strains in business partnerships, friendships, marriage, and parenthood. Assuming goodwill, friendship, and common goals in any of these types of relationships, I have seen that most of the strains boil down to one major issue—decision making.

Marie and Joe

Decisions must be made every day. On this particular day, Joe and Marie are sitting in their living room. Joe is about to break some good news to his wife.

Joe: I just got a three-hundred-dollar-per-month raise. Let's invest it in a new couch.

Marie: You got a raise? Hooray! (They melt into each other's arms, and after a few loving hugs and kisses, they resume the conversation.)

Marie: A new couch would be great, Joe. This one is looking pretty tired.

Joe: It sure is. Let's go look at some in the store.

(A few minutes pass by.)

Marie: Joe…?

Joe: I'm listening. (He gives her a big hug.)

Marie: When we go to my mom's house, it's sure great to shove the dishes in a dishwasher. One of those would save me lots of work. (Pause.) Let's get a dishwasher instead of a couch.

(There's a long stretch of silence.)

Marie: Joe? What are you thinking?

Joe: Why do you always contradict me? You know there's no room for a dishwasher in the kitchen. Besides, a couch will benefit the entire family, including you. Do we always have to differ over what to buy?

Marie: You don't have to get mad!

Joe: I'm not mad!

Well, Joe and Marie got worked up and their conversation over his raise ended in icy silence.

The next morning breakfast was a distasteful, uncomfortable, and silent ordeal. It was a relief to both of them when Joe left for work. That evening the air had cleared, supper was pleasant, and after the children were in bed, Joe and Marie had another discussion.

Joe: I'm sorry about my attitude last night.

Marie: Me too.

(They melt into each other's arms. For a moment there is no conversation.)

Joe: I've been thinking. I thought we could price a dishwasher and a couch.

Marie: That's plenty fair enough.

They went shopping together. They found out that a dishwasher would not fit in their kitchen. And couches were more expensive than they thought they would be; the old one would do fine for a few more years, especially since the children were small and had a tendency to jump on it and even accidentally spill things on it. So…they decided that for the time being a new couch would bring more problems than pleasure.

It is strange what happens to partners. Sensible people will come up with reasonable decisions.

Decisions, Decisions

Remember that mysterious stranger within? You find yourself feeling, thinking, saying, and doing the strangest things.

Why?

Joe and Marie had every intention of having a happy marriage, but they ended up in a cool silence over a decision.

Why?

Because of human nature. Remember the description of people that was noted in the last chapter? The apostle Paul said, "For the good that I will to do, I do not do; but the evil I will not to do, that I practice" (Romans 7:19).

Whenever two or more people must cooperate—no matter how dedicated, cooperative, or hardworking they may be—they will sooner or later get hung up over a decision and come to a stalemate. Everything that could be said will have been said, and all of the facts will be in, with nothing more to be added. Yet in spite of all of their good intentions, the partners will find themselves at a standstill.

A Matter of Opinion—But Whose?

Because it requires self-denial, decision making reveals another side of human nature and provides a wonderful opportunity for character development. The Bible describes the struggle like this: "We have turned, every one, to his own way" (Isaiah 53:6).

How true this statement is even today: If we are not living in a way that exhibits dying to our own will and living in His, our responses will be something like, "My ideas, my plans, my way sounds pretty good to me." The potential for conflict arises when the other person's way of doing things is different from ours and he also thinks his way is better. Even when partners are normally committed to harmonious relations, there will be times when each is convinced that his or her own choice is the best one.

Choosing whether or not to buy new appliances or furniture is probably a matter of opinion where there is no right or wrong choice. But whose opinion will determine the decision? The answer to this question is the key to successful partnerships.

Success in business, cooperation in marriage, or parenthood—none of these objectives are lofty enough to overcome the strong pull a person feels to go his own way, to do his own thing. "To do it my way" is the sweetest music to anyone's ears. So what do we do about this tendency? Here are some suggestions:

1. Admit the truth about ourselves ("I want my own way").
2. Confess it to the Lord.
3. Ask Him to cleanse us and give us a spirit of cooperation.

Here is a suggested prayer—remember that prayer is talking to God—to help you make those steps:

> *Dear Lord,*
> *I need Your help. My desire to push my own ideas drives me so hard that it tends to spoil my fellowship with other people. I recognize this drive within me and I need Your help to correct it. Please give me a spirit of cooperation.*

Who Has the Last Word?

So how are those hang-ups in the living room solved?

First of all, personal preparation is required. Each person involved in the decision needs a God-given spirit of cooperation.

Second, each person involved is committed to reach the objectives of the partnership.

Third, someone is designated in advance to have the last word. In a business, it is the president. And in parenthood, it is…

It is who…?

The Most Controversial Question

The answer to that question is one of the most controversial issues of our time. Marriages break up over this issue. Let's look in once more on

Joe and Marie to see how they handled this matter of decision making.

At first their discussion about buying a couch or a dishwasher ended up in icy silence. The question was not settled that night. It did not need to be. In fact, few questions require an immediate decision.

An icy silence is not the best way to end a discussion, yet it happened. After all, we are not talking about people who have already grown up into the likeness of Jesus Christ. Like anyone else, Joe and Marie are people who each tend to stand their own ground.

This is not the first time they had gotten hung up over a decision. In fact, they almost separated once because the need for making decisions piled up on them and became a contest instead of a cooperative effort.

Fortunately, they ran into someone who introduced them to Jesus Christ, and now Jesus is their Savior. They are learning to use God's Word, the Bible, to find clues on how to live together joyfully. Also, they asked Jesus to help them.

The Controversial Answer

They found an important truth from the Bible that saved their marriage. It was the answer to the most loaded of all questions: Who has the last word? They found one clue when they were furious with each other over some basic issues. They both worked outside of the home at the time, and these issues had stacked up:

- Who makes the bed?
- Who sweeps the floor?
- Who washes dishes?
- Should we get a red car or a blue car?
- What speed should we drive on the freeway? (She said sixty; he said seventy.)

Their friend, who introduced them to searching the Bible for clues, led them to what they thought was a bombshell.

The question was: How do you solve a hang-up? The biblical answer was: "Wives, submit to your own husbands, as to the Lord" (Ephesians 5:22).

When she read that, Marie hit the ceiling. "I'm not taking orders from him," she declared.

"Why not?" asked the friend.

"All he cares about is himself."

Marie was right about that statement; but of course, all she cared about was herself too. There is no way to succeed in a partnership between two people who are mad at each other and have no intention of cooperating.

Joe and Marie decided to try it God's way. They did not stop with that one controversial passage. They also meditated on, discussed, and prayed about the other Scriptures that form the context of that one Scripture:

> Therefore do not be unwise, but understand what the will of the Lord is. And do not be drunk with wine, in which is dissipation; but be filled with the Spirit, speaking to one another in psalms and hymns and spiritual songs, singing and making melody in your heart to the Lord, giving thanks always for all things to God the Father in the name of our Lord Jesus Christ, submitting to one another in the fear of God.
>
> Wives, submit to your own husbands, as to the Lord. For the husband is head of the wife, as also Christ is head of the church; and He is the Savior of the body. Therefore, just as the church is subject to Christ, so let the wives be to their own husbands in everything.

Husbands, love your wives, just as Christ also loved the church and gave Himself for her, that He might sanctify and cleanse her with the washing of water by the word, that He might present her to Himself a glorious church, not having spot or wrinkle or any such thing, but that she should be holy and without blemish.

So husbands ought to love their own wives as their own bodies; he who loves his wife loves himself. For no one ever hated his own flesh, but nourishes and cherishes it, just as the Lord does the church.

Ephesians 5:17–29

Even though the Scriptures listed above were Joe and Marie's objectives, their conversation about buying a couch had still ended up in icy silence.

What made the happy ending possible? During the day, Joe and Marie separately repented of drifting away from a God-given spirit of cooperation. They realized that they had allowed their own personal opinions to overshadow their partnership. The fruit of their repentance could be seen in how they treated each other with kindness and admitted their own faults. This made a loving conversation possible and resulted in their joyfully discovering new information that led to a decision they both agreed upon.

Saving Marriages

When honesty and goodwill prevail, most decisions will be settled in a mutually agreeable fashion. When there is a stalemate, someone must have the last word.

Joe and Marie decided to try the biblical way and found that God saved their marriage. When there is a stalemate, Joe settles it. But many times he depends on Marie's judgment, especially when the children are involved.

Sometimes they still drift back to their old ways of fighting over a decision, but when they realize what is happening, they return to the biblical way.

FAMILY LEADERSHIP

Betty, a thirty-six-year-old mother, announced one day: "If there is one scene I look forward to every day, it's when my husband, Bob, comes home from work.

"Sometimes the kids get to him in the driveway before I do; sometimes we all see him at once as he comes through the door. But no matter how many times we've gone through this routine, his arrival always perks up the day for the rest of us.

"Maybe we've had a bad day. Maybe it's been a good day. In either case, when he pops through that door, full of enthusiasm, sometimes with kids hanging all over him, I feel like saying just like they do on the talk shows: 'Now…Heeeeerrrrrre's Dad!'"

This is the way a family should be able to respond when Dad arrives on the scene. Obviously, this would not happen if he were tyrannical, failing to express the love of God to his children, or failing to love his wife as Christ loved the church and gave Himself for it. The presence of a dad, who is giving himself for others, will decorate the home with joy, peace, trust, and safety.

The Prosperous Farmer

Several years ago when I was the dean of a college, I visited a prosperous farmer whose son and daughter were students at my school. All the way to their parents' house, they spoke highly of their dad. I soon found out why.

After breakfast that first morning, I looked up and saw that the father was in the kitchen helping his wife with the dishes. A little later I glanced through the window and saw him washing his son's car. During the day the daughter used her dad's car, while he used the truck. Finally, I asked him why he was doing all of this.

"It's my way of saying a special 'thank you' to the kids for wanting to come back home. And I'm helping my wife so she has more time to spend with the kids."

This pattern continued the entire weekend. The mother and father slept on cots in the basement so the guests could have the best rooms in the house and the children could use their own rooms.

This man was no slave. He was not henpecked. This was not a daily occurrence in which he undertook all those tasks, but he was willing to pitch in on special days. He was not spoiling his children, nor was he ordered around or imposed upon.

His attitude was contagious though: Soon the children were helping him with the farm chores and pitching in to help with the housework.

Dad had set the tone. He was following the example of Jesus, who said of Himself, "'For even the Son of Man did not come to be served, but to serve, and to give His life a ransom for many'" (Mark 10:45).

Jesus also said that "'Whoever desires to become great among you shall be your servant'" (Mark 10:43).

Kindheartedness and benevolence makes working out the details of life simple. Without the expressions of love and cheerfulness, the activities of daily living can be empty and unrewarding.

Dad, Pay Attention to Us!

Not all dads are like this, however. Ralph, for instance, has this viewpoint. "When I come home, I figure my work is done. I'm home. And it's up to my wife and family to make me comfortable. After all, I'm the man of the house. I work all day and deserve a rest."

Another man, Ken, feels more or less the same way. His son floods him with an endless stream of questions as soon as he comes through the door. But Ken does not enthusiastically sweep his son into his arms because he is happy that his son was anxiously waiting for him to walk through the door. No, Ken has constructed a defense against his son's need for communication with his father. He sets his son down beside him and starts reading the evening paper while his son talks on. But Ken doesn't hear a word his son is saying.

Ken grunts out an occasional: "Uh-huh. No. Oh? Yes."

One evening this solid line of defense got him into trouble, though. On this night he had ignored nearly all of the boy's questions, then he suddenly "came to" right after he had incoherently grunted to the sound of one of his son's questions.

"What do you do all day down at your office?" the boy had asked.

Before he realized what his absentminded remark meant when it was put together with his son's question, the father impatiently shot out: "Oh, nothing."

After a thoughtful pause the boy asked, "Dad, then how do you know when you are through at work?"

This shows how literally and seriously the boy had taken his father's remarks. Evidently, it had not yet dawned on the boy that his father did not listen to him, or that his father only responded to him with empty, thoughtless words. Even though he had his son on the couch next to him, the father's mind was somewhere else. Being present in body is not enough. Parents must be present in both body and in spirit, and be honest with their children when they are not available to them. Otherwise, a trust between parent and child will be broken, and untold problems may result.

FAMILY PROCESSES

There are many similarities between running a business and running a family. In either organization the leader is fully responsible for ensuring the success of the organization. It is his task to see to it that plans, budgets, standards, and rules are set up. He must provide the supervision and training necessary for reaching the objectives.

WHAT A PRESIDENT DOES

Permit me to share with you how this worked in my company and then make comparisons to the family structure. We started from scratch, and over a period of five years we built a chain of six restaurants that employed 250 people. Some of my duties as president included:

1. setting the objectives
2. providing the finances
3. providing buildings and equipment
4. determining standards of quality and service
5. setting policies and rules
6. providing standards of performance
7. providing training and supervision
8. providing maintenance of property and equipment
9. providing cost controls
10. delegating responsibility and authority

I did not do this by myself. To manage six restaurants required one general manager, two assistants to the general manager, six managers, twelve assistant managers, and one office manager.

The standards, policies, procedures, and rules were not conceived by me and then handed down to the employees. They were created and changed primarily by daily interaction between the general manager and the manager.

You may wonder why it takes 22 people to manage 250 people. Remember, though, that some people are honest, cooperative, ambitious, unselfish, and dependable; but others are dishonest, undependable, uncooperative, lazy, and selfish. Plus, even the most wonderful people will sometimes come to work in a mood that will negatively affect the quality of their work. The task of the management staff is to maintain or restore goodwill, commitment, and cooperation.

The task can be summarized best by looking again at a Bible passage referred to in the last chapter: "Fulfill my joy by being like-minded, having the same love, being of one accord, of one mind. Let nothing be done through selfish ambition or conceit, but in lowliness of mind let each esteem others better than himself" (Philippians 2:2–3).

Cooperation requires continuous and ongoing discussion, review, and change among people of goodwill. This was especially true of the relationship between me and my general manager. In order for the general manager to implement my ideas with the managers and assistant managers, he had to know my mind and what I was committed to. I also needed to know his mind and accept his ideas and help implement them.

Look back at that verse again. Notice the two words: *like-mindedness* and *agreement*. Those attitudes are keys to the success of any good business or strong family.

SETTING UP THE FAMILY

How does this managerial model apply to the family? Parenthood may be viewed as a small business where the leaders are the husband and wife.

The family usually starts out small and grows gradually, somewhat like many businesses in America today. The duties of the family managers include, but are not limited to, the following duties:

1. setting the objectives
2. providing the finances
3. providing food and clothing
4. providing buildings and equipment
5. providing maintenance of property and equipment
6. guiding the children
7. determining standards of quality and service
8. setting policies and rules
9. providing standards of performance
10. providing training and supervision
11. providing cost controls
12. delegating responsibility and authority

See how similar this is to running a business? None of this is possible without a foundation of goodwill, commitment, and cooperation. To put it in biblical terms, we must submit to each other in the fear of God (see Ephesians 5:21).

To put it another way, the couple will design a harness that both of them will wear. This is not the same as a husband designing a harness for his wife to wear. Instead, this is a cooperative effort. Both wear the harness that includes, but is not limited to, the duties and responsibilities listed above.

What resources does a Christian couple have? Time, talent, ability, money, and their faith in God. Because it is somewhat like a small business, each manager is personally involved. There is a president and an executive vice president—and that is it.

The Officers

The husband is the president, even if the wife is more intelligent and efficient than her husband. To help clarify this, I will describe an example from my own business experience. In my company we had an employee who knew more about food than anyone else. Even so, he was not the president of the company just because he was more knowledgeable about food; however, because he was an employee who carried much responsibility and authority, he made many decisions on his own.

Managing the Family

How does a husband fulfill his role of managing a family? Since this book focuses on parenthood, I will select the topic of guiding children as an example.

When our children were still living at home with us, my wife and I were both deeply committed to guiding our children in the way they should go. Imagine with me for a moment one of the meetings that my wife and I had about child management. I am the president, and the family is my responsibility. My wife, who is the world's greatest expert on the subject of our children, is the executive vice president.

Together we set limits and provide supervision and training. How does a president proceed when he has the world's greatest expert on his hands? The answer seems obvious. He leans heavily on her expertise. One would be foolish to ignore such a person. Before you would contradict or overrule this person, you had better have a good reason.

This is exactly how we proceeded. I delegated the responsibility and authority for child guidance to my wife. Their feeding, clothing, education, social life, and duties were her responsibility. In other words, she told me how things were to be handled. I was not "copping out" here: I was wisely drawing upon the best talent available. You may not be able to structure duties in this same manner in your family. Work responsibilities and talents may require both parents to be active in those areas.

We did not have Eva's way of handling the children and Henry's other way of handling the children. Instead, we had a way that both of us were committed to. We had common guidelines, policies, and limits. Eva was in charge—whether I was at home or not. We were of the same mind.

Even though she was in charge, there was no doubt about who the president was. Yet Eva was the executive vice president with all the authority to act as needed. Just as in a business—policies, procedures, and limits kept changing. We were both committed to any changes that needed to be made. Personal involvement was required from both of us because continuous, ongoing conversation was needed just to keep up-to-date.

When goodwill, commitment, and cooperation undergird any organization, hang-ups seldom occur. Regardless of how your home responsibilities are distributed, cooperation is necessary. At our house, Eva was in charge.

United We Stand

Occasionally when I would come home at night, one of our children would come running out to me and say, "Dad, can I go out tonight?"

I was in the driveway, not even in the house yet. I was in no position to answer that question. Why? Because the person who had been in charge of this outfit all day long was in the house, and I had not consulted with her. That woman in the house was my friend. We were on the same management team. She was the authority. Along with that, she was executive vice president of the family. I would have been foolish to make decisions on behalf of our children without consulting her. In business, if I came to a restaurant and met the manager first, I did not give him an opinion on any big decision until I had first talked to the general manager.

Talking with my wife first was necessary before I could answer my children. I could not give them an answer when I first came home. To put it in the business vernacular, I did not have any data. Decision making without data, or guessing, may lead to trouble. In fact, a husband making a decision without data will probably have to change his decision immediately. Usually when I proposed to check with Eva, the child would say, "Don't bother." He or she had already checked with her.

A Business Meeting at Home

I had many meetings with the key person in my business. We sat down together to plan what was best for the future and evaluated what we had been doing in the past. We made some changes. We might even revise what we had been doing up until then.

The home should be the same. Marriage partners sit down and review the day, the week, or the interim time during which the husband or the wife has been away.

You can start from two basic questions:

1. What problems did you have that you were able to solve?
2. What problems did you have that you were unable to solve?

Maybe you will make some changes. The two of you may evaluate the rules again. The job here will be to chart the course for your family. Not two courses, but one. Not one way when Dad is home and another way when Mom is home. Many times I have heard children say, "I can get along okay with my dad when he is home and Mom is gone." Or, "I can get along all right with my mother when she is home and Father is gone, but when they are together it is difficult because my parents do not agree."

Agreement and unity comprise the foundation on which you build an effective family life.

If you function as president and executive vice president, you will discover that being in business for yourself—the family business—can be a lot of fun.

Note the word *if.* If there is goodwill, commitment, and cooperation, you can have fun. Remember we are talking about people, not angels. There were times when ill will, selfishness, stubbornness, and anger would more accurately describe one or both of us. Neither of us would repent. Such a spirit between us could last for days or weeks.

(Problem solving will cease as long as such a condition exists.)

Again, parenting will expose the soul. Each person must face the presence of that mysterious stranger—sin. When this happens, negotiation must be tabled. During this time it is important to remember that the only way to deal with sin is to look to God. No human being can help. Repentance before God that leads to forgiveness, cleansing, and yielding to the Holy Spirit's control is the only way to restore goodwill between spouses. Then, and only then, can the couple proceed to problem solving in a manner that glorifies God.

Of course, the love relationship between husband and wife is the key to a happy home where all family members enjoy, respect, and appreciate one another. That is why these chapters are included in a parenting book.

The husband and wife must be rightly related to God so they can be good parents and also be rightly related to one another. But keep in mind that if each individual parent is rightly related to God, it will be impossible to be wrongly related to one another. To understand this concept, we can look again at how Ephesians 5:21 states that husbands and wives should be "submitting to one another in the fear of God."

Good parenting will flow out of two individuals rightly related to God, loving one another with all their heart. This will make them great partners in marriage, parenting, or any other venture.

5

MOM—

MRS. EXECUTIVE

VICE PRESIDENT

THOUGHT STARTER

*A husband without a wife is not
the most effective organization.*

MEMORY VERSE

*Who can find a virtuous wife?
For her worth is far above rubies.*

PROVERBS 31:10

PROVERBS 31 IS AN INCREDIBLE CHAPTER. IT CONTAINS
an incredible list of characteristics, roles, and responsibilities. Can you
believe they are all found in the same woman?

Here is that list: seamstress extraordinaire, businesswoman, purchaser of goods, obtainer of food, time and schedule organizer, real
estate purchaser, physical fitness expert, teacher, ambitious, fears the
Lord, clothes purchaser, community worker, good citizen, social worker,
dietitian, good dresser, saleswoman, tireless, lets her job speak for itself,
praised by family and community alike. That is some kind of woman!
This is hardly someone who only keeps house.

Is it not a pity that we so often ignore the Bible? The roles and characteristics of the woman described in this chapter could serve as an outline for any awareness course about women.

Yet modern literature would have us believe that the tremendous talent and ability residing in women is a recent discovery. Any man who has not taken note of the fact that women are on par with men as intelligent, creative people just has not been paying attention.

A GOOD LESSON

Very early in life I learned about the competence of women. During my junior high school days, the local newspaper had a young writers' club. Our English teacher required all of us to write a weekly story for the club. She would pick the best story and send it to the paper for publication. Nine out of ten weeks, the best story was written by one of the girls.

Also, during those days I was put in charge of managing schoolwide candy sales to raise money for our extracurricular activities. The two top "salespersons" were always girls.

And I had another responsibility during my high school days that showed me something about women. I was assigned to be in charge of the mimeographing at the school. I started recruiting workers…some boys and some girls. Of the two groups, I soon found that the girls proved to be more efficient, trustworthy, and cooperative than the boys.

In college, the top student in my class was a girl. No matter what the rest of us did, she was always out there in front. Even so, being the top student in the class was not enough for her. She also was president of several leading clubs at the school.

As I made my way through the business and church worlds, I also noticed that a woman could direct a vacation Bible school just as well, if not better, than a man. Then in my restaurant business, the person we assigned to be in charge of the money was a woman.

I never cease to marvel at the skill and ease with which my wife can produce a delicious meal. The finest chef may match her skill, but I doubt if anyone could exceed her. To her, cooking is fun.

People often visit us for the express purpose of seeing me. They might spend eight hours with me and only a half hour with my wife (at a meal), but when they write us later, they all seem to remember my wife and her cooking most—not me and how I may have helped them.

THE CONSTANT COMPLAINT

On the other hand, Janie, age forty-four, wails:

> There must be more meaning to life than this! In the morning, my husband and the kids all descend upon the kitchen, where I feed them breakfast. At noon, part of that original crew returns to have their stomachs filled again. Then they all disappear and I don't see them again until early evening when they suddenly materialize just in time to have their tummies filled again. Why, all our kitchen is…is a filling station! And I'm the attendant.

Mary Ann, age twenty-eight, echoes similar sentiments:

> All through high school, my parents saved money for my college. I worked after school and during summers. Then, together, we struggled to pay my way through college. Finally, I received my degree. Then, after I completed college, instead of using that degree, I got married. Now, I change diapers, sweep the floors, cook meals, and wash dishes all day. Did I need a college degree for that? I've never felt so worthless in all my life.

Details can be wearisome, can't they? Have you ever thought about how many ear holes and nose holes a doctor examines each day? Does he think of his job in terms of nose holes—or in terms of healing people?

Ralph, who works in a kitchen-cabinet shop, sees himself as a craftsman of wooden works of art. Another employee in the same shop has a different outlook. He is a grumpy, crabby griper who only saws boards, inhales sawdust, and gets glue all over his fingers. Both do the same job. Both make beautiful cabinets.

What about the soggy mouths a dentist looks into during his working hours? Does he look at it as a job examining soggy mouths or helping people maintain good dental hygiene?

MR. EVERYTHING

Let's take a look at a unique situation: Valerie has a business of her own. Her husband, Erik, stays at home and does the housework. He sees the children off to school each day. He helps with the shopping and the cooking, but this still leaves lots of time on his hands.

Erik has become a volunteer worker at church—and a busy one at that. He is perfectly happy and loves his role. To meet Erik, you would think you had met the ideal man: Big. Handsome. Personable.

But Erik is a loafer. At one time he had a job that carried a lot of responsibility. Then came a demotion and then another. Finally he was fired—for laziness.

So Valerie, who is a competent and responsible person, stepped into the gap. She got a job and then started her own business. For ten years she has supported the family. Valerie's situation is exactly what some wives desire. She is free from the routines of managing a home.

But all is not well. She would rather be a homemaker. "It's not fair,

Dr. Brandt," she says. "I want to be home doing housework and taking care of the kids, but Erik won't let me."

There it is. According to my years of observation in the counseling room, I have found that the basic cause of marital discord is conflict and ill will between couples. The routines must be handled, no doubt about that. But the debate is about, "who does what." For Erik and Valerie, it is a standoff. It has been a ten-year debate. No one has the last word, so the issue cannot be settled.

Women and men need to be effectively and happily engaged in activities that they find to be a fulfilling way of releasing the unique gifts God designed them to release. Contentment does not come by dropping one set of routines for another, though. Erik and Valerie found that out.

The division of responsibilities between a husband and wife is, of course, negotiable. A couple can only come to mutually agreeable decisions as both parties are committed to the mutual interests of one another and a final authority is established.

In this example we see that Eric is a loafer and is not doing the right thing. But the situation cannot be resolved if both of them do not work at it. There is a debate going on that they will not solve unless they work as a team—as partners, not opponents.

However, another major point here is that Valerie must learn to be content even if her husband is doing the wrong thing. True, Eric needs to get up and go to work. But if he chooses not to, Valerie must deal with her own heart. She can walk in the Spirit in the midst of this difficulty, or she can walk in the flesh. Walking in the Spirit will not solve Erik's problem, but it will give her what she needs to walk through a difficult time. If she walks in the Spirit and exhibits fruits that display a close relationship with the Lord, she will be more effective in every area of her life.

THE SWIMMING INSTRUCTOR

Sarah had a lot of extra time on her hands even though she was managing a household that included her four children ages two through fourteen and a husband who was in business for himself.

"I don't have any big trouble with the children," she said. "I host the parties for Edgar when he's entertaining. I take care of the house. I help out with the business. Still, I've got a lot of time on my hands that I don't want to spend vegetating in front of the television."

So she and her husband decided that volunteering to teach a swimming class at the YMCA would be a great match for her schedule, talent, and interests. It was not that she hated housework or managing children. But she had time on her hands and a busy mind. Her husband wholeheartedly encouraged her, plus the babysitting service at the YMCA enabled her to take the baby with her to her class.

Sarah was good—so good that within a year she was teaching four courses at the YMCA. Even though she was now spending a total of about ten hours on four different days at the Y, she still easily managed to meet her primary responsibilities as wife and mother. Sarah could have become bored. But, while balancing her primary goals beautifully, she went out and devoted her extra time to activities that benefited her community and provided a means for her to release her talents and gifts in other ways. Not every wife and mother wants to work or be involved in community activities outside the home. Each husband and wife must make a decision as to what is right for their family.

THE GIRL WHO WAS TOPS IN HER CLASS

The same was true of Linda. A very creative person, she had graduated from college at the top of her class and then immediately married. She eventually had two children, but she was becoming bored. She suggested to her husband that they start a children's program for their small church, which had trouble recruiting leaders.

"But I want to do a good job," she said when she suggested the idea to him.

"I'm all for it. Let's go," he replied.

Together, they threw themselves into the task and came up with a unique program for children ages three to twelve in their church.

She helped plan the weekly schedule. To enhance the children's programs, she found special films to show to the children and invited guest speakers to minister to them. She added special touches by doing artwork, setting up puppet stages, and even starting a Christian book-reading program.

The children's program helped turn the entire trend of the church around. The church had been losing families who had elementary-age children. Now, the families stayed and the church grew. Others heard about the program and wanted to know more.

The church was so delighted that on Linda's birthday they sent her a beautiful bouquet of flowers with the note, "Happy birthday! From the parents of Grace Church."

Also, the two of them decided Linda was the better storyteller of the team. So she has been telling a series of stories for the weekly gatherings. She then began working on the project of making some of the stories into books. It would not have happened if Linda and her husband had not recognized the need in their church and then determined that they had the time and talents for meeting needs outside of their own home.

HAPPINESS REQUIRES TEAMWORK!

Then, there's Margie. She is a bitter, resentful woman who constantly gripes about her home and her husband. She, too, is a volunteer worker. She is a driver with the Red Cross.

If a person needs to go downtown to get a welfare check, or someone gives blood and then passes out, or an elderly person needs to go to the hospital for vital shots—Margie drives them.

She does not enjoy her work for one minute. She gripes about the "miserable people." She gripes just as much as she does about her home and husband.

Two volunteers—Linda and Margie. Why are they so different? They have two different problems. Linda had a desire to use her time wisely. Margie needs to experience a new relationship with Jesus Christ.

Staying busy, even in volunteer work, does not take care of your spirit. You must make a distinction between dealing with your spirit and dealing with the untapped use of your talent and intelligence.

Two Professors

When I was going to college, I met a professor who was the main influence on my views of parenthood. Her name was Ethel Waring, and she was an incredible person. She was happy. She was radiant. She was an inspiring college professor. What made her that way? Simple. She was a happy woman.

I know another woman who is a college professor. Her reason for teaching is not so she will be of service or contributing to the lives of others. She is teaching to get away from her husband, whom she hates. Her college teaching has not made a happy woman out of her, because it is a means of escape from another situation that she refuses to solve. In fact, her busyness has made her even unhappier, for she keeps comparing her husband (who is really a nice, competent guy) with some of the other male professors. She goes home and often takes potshots at her husband.

What is she doing? She is multiplying her misery not only by being a hateful woman toward her husband, but also by being a phony at work.

Talents Must Be Combined with Godly Attributes

Competence, intelligence, and organizational ability: These are characteristics of both men and women that need to be expressed. However, this expression alone does not change the spirit of the man or the woman. Some men and some women waste their talents because they do not combine them with godly attributes, such as love, joy, peace, long-suffering, kindness, goodness, faithfulness, gentleness, and self-control (see Galatians 5:22–23).

MEET THE VP

In most businesses, the two top officers are the president and the executive vice president. The president oversees the company and helps establish the main plan and policies for the company. He may travel many different places to represent the company.

When it comes to the day in and day out running of the business, the executive vice president is usually the key officer. The executive vice president really makes things run smoothly. Although the president may be responsible for many final decisions, he rarely makes a decision without leaning heavily on the advice of someone in the company, usually the executive VP, who is a very knowledgeable, authoritative person in his own right. These individuals are friends and sense a high degree of accomplishment as they work together. It is difficult to distinguish one's input from the other.

This is a perfect description of the roles of a father and a mother. While dad might be known as the head of the home and is responsible for many of the ultimate decisions, he probably does not manage the daily activities of the home. The mother often does that. No matter what the structure of duties in the home, the wife is the executive vice president. Her influence is enormous, and her wisdom is one of the most important assets of the organization.

Such an authoritative person (an expert) makes decisions, as necessary, within the policies of the organization—without consulting anyone. Many women can easily manage the family and still have much time to spare.

THE FAMILY PLAN

When my wife and I first started out in this business of raising a family, we got together and listed all of *our* responsibilities. (Notice I said *our* responsibilities, not *my wife's* responsibilities or *my* responsibilities.)

Just a few of the many we detailed were: housecleaning, money management, cooking, writing, radio work, children, cleaning the yard, travel plans, running a business, raising money, and purchasing food.

Then we divvied them up—she handled the money management, travel plans, housecleaning, cooking, children, food purchasing, and a bunch more. I was assigned writing, radio work, cleaning the yard, running a business, and raising money. The duties were designated according to training, ability, interest, and necessity.

How we met the responsibilities was not the question. The assignment was simple. These were the responsibilities each of us was to carry out. If my wife decided to add responsibilities outside the home, fine. But she would first have to figure out some way to carry out her primary tasks. The same went for any other activities I took on. Adding more activities outside the home was fine as long as I kept the primary activities going. Of course, they kept changing as the children grew and demands on our time changed.

In all our planning and assigning, we kept one thing in mind—our plans must be a family plan. We made sure to remember that it was the Brandt plan—not Henry's plan or Eva's plan. It was our plan, and we committed to carry out our responsibilities.

Many decisions can and should be made without involving the president of a company or the husband in a family. To illustrate this point, I will refer to another business model.

A meeting is being held in a business. Present are the general manager (the number two person in the organization), two assistants, and six managers. The question under discussion is a "letdown" in five of the restaurants on uniform cleanliness and crispness.

"I'll admit it," says one of the managers. "We have eased our enforcement of this, but only because of the policy."

"Right," says another manager. "If we follow the policy and send an employee home every time he reports to work with a uniform that isn't neat, then he gets mad and threatens to quit.

"And business is booming so much, that if we are short even one waiter or waitress because of such a policy, it really cuts into our ability to give the people good service," he continues.

"No good service, no good business," adds another.

"I disagree," exclaims one of the assistants. "We've always held to a standard of cleanliness, right?"

Everyone agrees.

"Well, if we start allowing our uniforms to get sloppy, the entire operation begins to get sloppy. Relax a standard here and then a standard there. Pretty soon, we're sloppy all around. And then we'll really lose customers."

The debate is now on. After a little more discussion, it is obvious that the group is hopelessly split. It is time for the general manager to make a decision. The neat-uniform policy will stand. Everyone accepts it and that is that.

After the meeting is over, the general manager calls me and gives me a verbal report. The decision has been made because the president had already given this authority to the general manager. The general manager's record of performance, and the fact that he has firsthand contact with the managers, had been the basis for the president's decision to delegate this authority.

"I've Made Some Changes around Here!"

A family organization is much smaller than a restaurant chain, of course. In the family situation, there is a president and an executive vice president, or man and wife. Let's take a look at Joe and Marie again because they will provide us with a fine example of a father supporting his wife's decisions.

Joe and Marie are sitting at the kitchen table. Their two boys, ages eight and ten, are playing outside.

Marie: I made some changes around here.

Joe: What are they?

Marie: I've pushed bedtime up a half hour, and also the kids must take their shoes off on the landing.

Joe: Okay.

That night, Joe puts the children to bed. This was normally Marie's job, but she was too tired and asked him to do it. Each boy griped to Dad because he had to take his shoes off on the landing. Their father's response to them was, "That's the way it is."

Go, Team, Go!

Guiding children is the responsibility of the organization. Joe and Marie are a team. They work together. They care about each other. Of course he will put the children to bed if she is tired. He may put them to bed often. The pattern of responsibilities is a negotiable matter. There is no competition here, just cooperation.

What else does Marie do besides keeping house and managing the children? Whatever she and Joe agree on is reasonable. What else does Joe do besides his income-producing job? Whatever he and Marie agree on is reasonable. Agreement is the key word. It is a team effort. On the other hand, unresolved conflicts are the soil for weak marriages.

Nancy Wanted a Washing Machine

Nancy and Kevin could not agree on who should control the money. They also had other areas where they held differing opinions. There were many verbal barrages. She wanted a washer and dryer. He said she would get them only over his dead body. Her response was to buy them.

In retaliation, Kevin went on a drinking spree that lasted several days. Out of spite, he bought a new station wagon. Nancy did not enjoy her appliances. They were a rebuke to her every time she used them. Nor did her husband enjoy driving that new station wagon.

Here were two people who had acquired some equipment that should have given them joy and satisfaction. Instead, these useful things were a bone of continuing contention. Behind the strife over money was the unsettled question of submission. Both persons were asserting a spirit of independence and selfishness. They were hardly a team.

Two Voices—One Tune

One day my daughter came to me and said, "The church youth group is going roller skating. Can I go?"

I was not in a position to make that decision. So I simply checked with my wife, who replied, "Well, the condition for going roller skating was that she have her homework done."

"That's right," I added, "we agreed on that."

"Well, she doesn't have it done."

That was simple; case dismissed. However, this is not what happened in another family. Carole had asked her mother if she might go roller skating with the church group and Mom replied, "No, you were at prayer meeting last night, and you studied late the night before."

"Ah, let her go," Dad cut in. "She's only young once."

"But Carole needs her rest," Mom insisted.

Then the seesaw argument began, and both mother and father were soon angry. The incident was a common one in Carole's life. As a result, her head and heart spun with confusion and revolt, so much so that she eventually came to me for help.

This is deadly. Frequently the husband has one plan and the wife another. When the husband goes away to work, the wife says to herself, "Finally…he's gone! Now we can get back to normal around here."

It is so important for parents to speak with two voices—but with only one tune. Remember Joe and Marie? The decision to work in unison led to much joy and lots of fun for the whole family.

Call of the Beauty Shop

Another time, Joe and Marie agreed to go camping. Finding a time to go proved difficult. Joe wanted to go this weekend, but Marie had a beauty-shop appointment Saturday afternoon. After some discussion about canceling her appointment, Joe realized it would be an unnecessary nuisance for her. He could not go the following week, so they planned to go camping in three weeks. This kind of situation is no big deal among friends who really care about each other.

When they did go, they were all together on the project. At the camp site, Marie became acquainted with the lady in the tent next door. Marie was enjoying frying hamburgers beside the lake. But her neighbor was griping about being dragged away from home to endure the nuisance of outdoor cooking.

They were in the same spot with similar equipment, both cooking beside a lake. The difference was in the spirit of the women and their relationships with their husbands.

I would like to share a few sentences from another book we wrote, called *Marriage God's Way*, that further describes how a happy marriage is a lifelong process:

> A happy marriage involves a much greater challenge than simply finding a partner with whom you live happily ever after. It is more than some strange chemistry that draws and holds you together forever. Soon after the wedding day you realize that marriage is a test of your character. A happy marriage does not depend on perfectly matched partners. It is a lifetime process dependent on many choices made by two free individuals who deliberately choose the same harness and who continuously sacrifice personal freedom and self-interest for a mutually agreeable way of life.

NOW...THE CHILDREN

We are finished talking about the man now. And we are finished talking about the woman. We are assuming that the man and woman are content. So let's get on with the job of parenthood.

Again, each family should have as its goal to "Train up a child in the way he should go, and when he is old he will not depart from it" (Proverbs 22:6).

This is not a woman's job or a man's job: It is the task of the partnership. Assuming goodwill, friendship, and commitment, two highly competent people will get on with the job and have fun doing it together. If you were to sum up the content of the last chapter and this chapter in one word, that word would be *submission*. What we mean by this is a man and a woman submitting to a mutually acceptable and agreeable plan for guiding the affairs of the family—it is like wearing a two-part harness.

When a decision is to be made and the facts involved lead a couple to a stalemate, the husband will settle it—after careful consideration of his wife's recommendations. He should have some very good reasons if he overrules her judgment. In order to understand this in biblical terms, I encourage you to once again read Ephesians 5:21–28.

6

THE FOUNDATION FOR DISCIPLINE— LOVE AND CONVICTION

THOUGHT STARTER

All forms of discipline should rest on the foundation of love.

MEMORY VERSE

Love suffers long and is kind; love does not envy; . . . bears all things, believes all things, hopes all things, endures all things.

1 CORINTHIANS 13:4, 7

GOD'S WORD INSTRUCTS US TO LOVE ONE ANOTHER earnestly from the heart (see 1 Peter 1:22). Of course, this wonderful guideline applies to all relationships, including how parents should relate to their children. Nearly every parent wants to give his or her children tender, loving, and sacrificial care that flows out of a heart of love; but even the most dedicated mother or father cannot do this unless God is the source of that love. This is because God is love, and as we walk in His love—rather than in our sinful nature—His love will flow to our children through us.

God does not leave us without guidance. In fact, the biblical standard for love is described in 1 Corinthians 13:4–8. It has fourteen components:

- suffers long
- is kind
- does not envy
- does not parade itself
- is not puffed up
- does not behave rudely
- does not seek its own
- is not provoked
- thinks no evil
- does not rejoice in iniquity, but rejoices in the truth
- always bears all things
- believes all things
- hopes all things
- endures all things

God is love, and He is the source of all love. All good things flow from Him. Love is not something we can work up; it is something we receive from Him. Love is a spiritual matter and not just a set of attributes we try to display. Along with this, love is not merely a body of actions that parents do. Actions do not necessarily equate to the presence of love, because actions may be performed without love being the reason for the activities. Indeed, actions may be executed out of a sense of duty or need for conformity, or as a means of achieving personal gain.

Therefore, love is not something we do; it is something within us. For example, hugs, kisses, and generous deeds are only empty motions if they do not flow out of a loving spirit. Here is how one man describes the difference between empty actions and affectionate expressions of love: "I kiss my wife good-bye, but her lips are hard." The husband knows his wife is going through the motions of kissing him, but her heart is not with him. He senses that although she may be physically present, love is not present in her gesture. It follows then that if God is love and love is not present in her kiss, then the Spirit of God must not be at the center of the wife's relationship with her husband.

Just as a husband and wife can go through the motions of dutiful displays of affection, parents can respond to their children in pretentious ways. For example, a father may kiss his children when they come home from school out of a sense of obligation but at the same time he resents having the responsibilities of being a father.

Do children know the difference between actions that are motivated by a loving spirit and a set of empty procedures? Certainly they do. They may not be able to verbalize what they know in their hearts to be true, but they will respond to the emptiness all the same.

LOVE SHOULD NOT BE WITHDRAWN

We must also keep in mind that love must not be withdrawn. In the example of the man who says his wife's lips are hard when he kisses her, we can deduct that he is longing for the love she has withdrawn from him. Maybe she is bitter about something she thinks he has done to her. Maybe she is resentful about having to remain in her marriage commitment. Whatever the circumstances, there is absolutely no justification for withdrawing love. To do this is to no longer welcome the Holy Spirit into the relationship. When this happens, people are hurt and God's purposes cannot be accomplished.

Parents' love must be constant and unconditional. It should not be conditional or related to the children's behavior in any way. Just like we must be able to rest in God's love for us as we grow and mature in Him, children must be able to rest in their parents' love. For children to grow up healthily and confidently, moving peacefully along the pathway of God's perfect plan for their lives, they must be secure in their parents' love for them.

Love can (and should) be the basis from which parents operate when they help their children learn and consistently repeat appropriate behavior. Even guiding children away from unacceptable behavior can be accomplished with ease when love is the parents' motivation.

In any given situation that involves guiding children, adults will be forced to make decisions about how they will respond to their children and their actions. There will be many possibilities to choose from, many of which would not be beneficial to the children. Only a heart of love and reliance on God for His love and wisdom will consistently lead (and constrain) the adult to respond in ways that are mindful of the children's developmental level and truly in their best interests. One example comes to mind that illustrates this point well. The episode involving Terry and his child-care teachers shows the necessity for love to be at the very core of training children.

TERRY AND THE TRICYCLE

His teachers had recently made good progress helping Terry learn that biting other children was not the "right way" to get "his way." In fact, he had not bitten anyone for a long time. Then early one morning, Terry was quite sleepy and crabby when his mom dropped him off at the day-care center. The sun was so bright that he put his hands over his eyes and peeked through his fingers as he trudged out to the play-ground. Then suddenly, something shiny and red caught his eye. There it was. The tricycle was glistening in the sun, just waiting for him to hop on. But oh no, now there was a problem. Jose seemed to come out of nowhere. He suddenly made a mad dash for the tricycle and hopped on it just seconds before Terry could get to it. "Hey, I saw it first," Terry yelled. But Jose didn't look back as he tried to pick up speed and get away from Terry as fast as he could.

But Terry was too quick for Jose. Terry grabbed the handlebars so fast that Jose and the tricycle almost tipped over. Terry saw his chance when Jose was off balance, but his strategy didn't work because Jose regained control of the tricycle so quickly that Terry didn't have time to push him off the seat. Frustrated and convinced that the tricycle was his—because, after all, he had seen it first—Terry could only think of one way to stop Jose in his tracks, so in a split second he…. Yes, you guessed it.

The moment Terry bit Jose on the shoulder, he knew he had done the wrong thing. Jose cried out so loudly that everyone on the playground, including Terry, suddenly froze. Terry didn't think he had bitten Jose all that hard, but the way Jose was screaming and crying scared Terry so much and made him feel so bad about what he had done that he started crying too.

Within seconds, two teachers had dashed to the scene, Terry was crying uncontrollably, and Jose was still screaming as loudly as he possibly could.

The teachers now had a challenge on their hands. How would they react? Would they be angry, disgusted, and furious? Or would they treat each child kindly, tenderly, and compassionately? Their own spirits, not how the children had behaved, would determine the choices these teachers would make.

I am happy to say that they were kind, tender, and compassionate to both boys. One drew Jose aside to comfort him and find out what had happened. The other teacher drew Terry into a corner to ask him what had happened and to comfort him. "I forgot," Terry explained. The teacher reminded him that when he bit people, he hurt them. She also reminded him that biting people was not allowed. Terry would not be allowed to go back into the play area for a little while. He would be given time to think about what he should do next time another child had something he wanted. She made a mental note to watch him more closely for the rest of the day. It was clear that he would need extra help because he was tired and may have a hard time coping during some of the other activities throughout the day.

Was this enough? Was it enough just to tell Terry what he should not do? This is where many parents and caregivers stop. They often tell children they were wrong. They often tell children what they should not do. However, they should not stop there, because telling children what they should not do does not necessarily translate into telling them what they should do. If Terry needed help remembering what he should do the next time he got into that type of situation, then the caregiver would need to give him some suggestions. It may have been necessary for the teacher to remind Terry that he needed to ask a child nicely if he could use his tricycle for a while, and if the boy said no, Terry would either need to find another tricycle or choose something else to do. Also, Terry may have needed to be reminded to apologize to Jose for biting him. If Terry did not know the words to use to do this, the teacher would have needed to help him. The key here is to give the child the best possible chance for future success.

What followed was one of those moments that warms every teacher's heart. A few minutes after Terry was allowed to return to the playground, he walked up to the teacher and said, "Will you help me get a tricycle, please?" Asking her to do this indicated that he recognized the need for her help and that he felt he could trust her to give it to him. The situation would certainly have turned out much differently if the teacher had initially treated Terry insensitively when she had discovered that he had bitten yet another child. When she approached the situation, she could have responded much differently than she did. For example, she could have glared at him and shouted, "Didn't we tell you that you can't bite anyone?" However, if she had done this, her own biting words would have given him the wrong message. In essence, she would have been modeling a different form of violence.

Instead, because she had responded in love, God turned a difficult situation around by using this teacher to create a loving moment for the child, and now the child was creating a loving moment for her. When we review this situation, we see that the teacher had a loving spirit when she responded to Terry.

What should she have done if she saw the situation and recognized that she did not have a loving spirit toward Terry? My answer may surprise you. However, my answer is an important one because parents sometimes face similar situations. If the teacher knew she did not have a loving spirit toward Terry, she should have asked another teacher to help Terry. Asking another teacher to take care of Terry would have been a way of protecting Terry from being injured by her. Terry was in a different kind of pain than Jose was, but in that moment, Terry needed as much love as Jose did.

GENTLE FIRMNESS AND HOSTILE FIRMNESS

Unfortunately, many parents and caregivers excuse their own bad behavior by blaming their own actions on the behavior of the children. However, children and teens should not be controlling the emotions of the adults. It is the adult's responsibility to be Christlike in every situation, regardless of how the child is behaving.

However, I do want to point out that love does not mean inaction or allowing children to take charge of the adults. And it does not mean that the adult withdraws from fulfilling his or her responsibilities. The adult must lovingly help, guide, or redirect the child who misbehaves. Even a child's most obnoxious conduct may be dealt with in a gentle but firm way.

What is the difference between gentle firmness and hostile firmness?

Your spirit. You know the difference—and so does your child.

Because it is not born out of love, hostile firmness will injure the child. There are many ways for an adult to, in a spirit of hostility and anger, strike a child. These unbridled reactions may take the form of physical slaps and blows that are administered violently and mindlessly. Or the child may be stricken down with sharp words or stinging silence. Certainly, God has placed these children in our care, and this is not what He wants the children to receive from us. If this is what the children are receiving from our hands and from our mouths, then this is what they are receiving from our hearts.

If our hearts are full of hostility, we will give hostility to our children. In turn, if our hearts are full of love, we will give them love. When our spirits are full of love because we have received love from God, our children will learn and experience the nature of Jesus Christ—who dwells and reigns in us. When Jesus Christ reigns in the hearts and lives of the parents, the home will be a safe place in which the children can flourish and grow.

Just as Jesus Christ is the same yesterday, today, and forever, our love for our children must remain constant. Our children must be able to rely on our consistency in the same way that we rely and put our trust in the fact that Jesus Christ does not change. We cannot act lovingly one day and then act hatefully the next. That is why parenting cannot just be a role we play: Parenting must be an expression of our loving spirits. Love is not dependent upon the child's behavior, and it is not changed by the problems or circumstances the parent may face.

Admittedly, none of us is perfect. None of us is completely dead to the sinful nature of men and women who need the Savior, whose minds must be renewed in Christ Jesus and whose inward man must be renewed day by day (see Ephesians 4:23; 2 Corinthians 4:16b). All parents will have those moments of desperation when they must call out to God in their time of need.

DO NOT RESPOND WITHOUT LOVE

What then shall we do when a hostile spirit grips us and we react in selfish ways that hurt our children and other people around us?

We must repent—we must turn from our sinful ways. We must ask God for His forgiveness and His grace. And yes, something else is required. We must admit to our children that we were wrong, and if other people have been affected by our hostility, we must confess our fault to them. We must also ask those we have injured to forgive us. This will concretely show them that we are seeking to obey God's Word. It will also make it very clear that the type of behavior we exhibited is not something that should be copied. This example of humility will touch their hearts and lives, and strengthen our relationships with them.

This is the time for retracing our steps to find out what led up to the outburst. Oftentimes during this prayerful time of self-examination, God will show us that somehow we have been neglecting our relationship with Him. When we center our focus on Him and again submit our ways to His, our repentance and renewed relationship with Him will yield the fruits of righteousness. Every area of our lives will reflect our rediscovery of how His love flows through us so much more easily when our hearts are wholly devoted to Him and His purposes. As we join in closer partnership with Him, our confidence in our ability to parent our children in a way that glorifies Him will be restored. As we submit complete control over every area of ourselves and our lives to God, we must also ask Him to heal those we have injured. Then we must ask Him to guide us into opportunities where we can be vessels through which His healing and love flows more freely each day.

The apostle Peter points to a clear correlation between loving others and purifying our souls. He says, "Since you have purified your souls in obeying the truth through the Spirit in sincere love of the brethren, love one another fervently with a pure heart" (1 Peter 1:22).

Discipline with Love

You may be a parent who is full of questions about how to guide your children. Be encouraged by the fact that these very questions are a reflection of your love for your children. Some of your questions may include tough ones like:

- Should I withdraw my love when I punish my child?
- After I punish my child, should I show her that I love her?
- Should I withdraw affection from my child in order to keep him in line?

A Mother Discovers Love

Examining the family dynamic described below may help provide answers to these questions. After her daughter Carole had run away several times, Mrs. Jamesy brought her to me to see if I could help them. I soon discovered that Carole thought her mother was a cruel person. Mrs. Jamesy had been slapping Carole or pulling her hair if she dallied at doing her homework or washing the dishes. For as long as Carole could remember, her mother had used threats or punishments as means of trying to force Carole to behave and follow her mother's orders.

In bitterness, Carole did the direct opposite of everything her mother told her to do. Even though the young girl was a Christian, she deliberately disobeyed her mother.

You may be surprised by the fact that, despite her harshness with her daughter, it was obvious to me that Mrs. Jamesy truly wanted to be a good mother. However, Mrs. Jamesy thought it would be harmful for her to be friendly or affectionate when Carole misbehaved. Because she thought it was "bad" to express love to Carole when she was misbehaving, Mrs. Jamesy did not turn to God for love during the times when it was needed most. Because of this, love was not ruling her actions and bridling her words.

I helped Mrs. Jamesy see that withdrawing her love from Carole was causing her daughter to question her mother's love for her. The harshness and conflict that were produced during these violent scenes were like heavy, dark clouds that overshadowed their relationship. However, Mrs. Jamesy soon began to realize why Carole rebelled so easily. She also began to see that returning bitterness for bitterness was fueling rebellion in her daughter's heart.

I assured her that continuing to feel affectionate toward a child who is rebelling does not contradict a parent's goals for maintaining high standards for her child. After Mrs. Jamesy came to this realization, the tense atmosphere in their home was quickly transformed (by the Spirit of God) into an environment of love and understanding. Carole softened, and now both appreciate and enjoy a God-directed love that binds them closely together.

Here are answers to a few questions that may have come to your mind when you were reading about Mrs. Jamesy and her daughter:

- How much bad behavior should I endure before I withdraw my love? Never withdraw your love.
- How much stubbornness in my child would justify my bursting into anger? Bursting out in anger is never justified.
- Where is the line? There is no line.

The answer to all of these questions may be summed up in one statement: If your love breaks down, you need to repent. To understand this, we can look at this concept in another way:

- Does your bad behavior cause God to withdraw His love from you? No.
- Does God burst into anger because of what you have done? No.

- Does God draw a line that prohibits you from returning to Him? No.
- Does God correct, rebuke, chasten, and discipline those He loves? Yes.

The Lord Chastens Those He Loves

Because Hebrews 12:5–6 tells us the Lord chastens those He loves, this passage of Scripture implies that discipline and correction are actually expressions of His love for us. Just as God's love is not withdrawn from us when we are corrected by Him, we must not withdraw our love from our children when we discipline them. Instead, correcting and disciplining them should be an outflow from a heart of love. It should be an expression of love we have received from God.

Does this mean that our children will enjoy being corrected by us? No. Being corrected is not pleasurable; however, when it is an expression of our loving spirit, it will ultimately yield good fruit in them…and in us. As the writer of Hebrews says, "Now no chastening seems to be joyful for the present, but grievous; nevertheless, afterward it yields the peaceable fruit of righteousness to those who have been trained by it" (Hebrews 12:11).

A Loving Spirit

Obviously, the times when parents must chasten their children are not happy experiences for the ones receiving—or giving—the correction. However, parents must look beyond the present pain.

This brings us to the point that many parents are just too self-centered to correct their children. While they may say to themselves that they are "going easy" on the children, they may only be "going easy" on themselves. Parents are not doing their children any favors when they do not discipline them. In fact, parents' failure to correct their children is a form of withdrawing love.

Your task is not to keep your child smiling today at any price. Instead, God has allocated you with the responsibility of helping your child become a mature and responsible person who loves the Lord with a whole heart. By having a loving spirit when difficult situations arise, you are guiding your child with your love and leading him or her to the source of all love.

Praise for a job well done reassures a child. Admonition for a job poorly done lets him know he is not learning well. However, the actions of praising someone are not necessarily evidences of love for that person. For example, we can be filled with jealousy or animosity toward the person we have just praised for having performed a beautiful solo. On the other hand, admonishing someone is not evidence of the presence of love either. For example, we may resent time spent away from our favorite activity when we half-heartedly (or too harshly) admonish a child for doing a poor job of cleaning his room.

When you reflect on the examples above, the following question may come to mind: Does love and affection have to be present in me when I correct my child? Absolutely! Before admonishing your child, ask yourself the following questions: Can I correct my child with love? Can I correct my child with affection? If not, wait until you can.

In the following example we see what happened when a mother took disciplinary action too hastily.

Three Boys and a Dozen Eggs

One morning a mother of three children hummed happily to herself as she walked into the kitchen. Her three boys were huddled together around the kitchen sink and chattering happily. She thought, *My, they're getting along nicely this morning.* Then her pleasant feelings quickly turned to dismay when she caught a glimpse of what was on the counter. She couldn't believe her eyes when she realized the boys had piled a dozen eggshells next to a bowl of raw eggs.

This young mother was enraged. She angrily lectured the boys and told them they would have to stay isolated in the house all day long. She did not take time to find out what had transpired. She only assumed the worst. She did not take into consideration that they had stumbled on a discovery activity. Apparently, one of the boys had come up with the idea that he would poke a hole in the end of a raw egg, empty it out, and make a joke of throwing the empty eggshell at his mother when she walked into the kitchen. He had probably chuckled to himself when he imagined how shocked his mother would be when he threw what would look like a whole egg at her. He also knew they would all laugh together when she discovered that the egg white and yoke had been removed and he had only thrown an empty shell at her to make her laugh. The boys, however, found that emptying the contents of the egg was so interesting that they took out the contents of another egg, and another, and another until they had gone through a whole dozen eggs.

Apparently things did not go as the boy had planned; however, the mother did begin to think more rationally after she began calming down from her angry tirade. The more she thought about it, the more she realized she had overreacted. Here she was enraged, spoiling the day for herself—and for her children—over a dollar's worth of eggs. She realized she had responded irrationally, so much so that she regretted her hasty and thoughtless reaction.

First, she repented before the Lord, and then she called her children together to tell them that she was sorry she had exploded at them. Of course, she was sure to add that they would need to ask for her permission before they attempted to do any more science experiments. Everyone was relieved, and peace in the home was restored. And Mom made sure the eggs did not go to waste. They had scrambled eggs for lunch *and* for an afternoon snack!

From this example we can see how hasty responses can lead to mis-understandings or overreactions that hurt other people. As I noted earlier, however, there will be times when a parent does and says things he or she later regrets. In those cases, the parent can choose to go on like his or her actions were perfectly justified, or the parent can exhibit an example of humility and love. Yes, in the situation described above, the mother did overreact to the situation, but soon afterwards she corrected her mistake. She not only reconsidered her actions and repented before the Lord, but also called her children together and admitted to them that she had been wrong. By telling them that she had acted in a way that was inappropriate, she was telling them that this was not a type of behavior they should exhibit in their own lives. Her actions were a wonderful example of true repentance. She repented before God, admitted fault and apologized to her children, and then lovingly cared for them for the rest of the day.

Now let's look in on another family. This example shows the importance of being one who loves, instead of one who only acts lovingly.

A Home Healed by Love

There were ongoing conflicts between Mrs. Gordons and her daughter, Betty. During our first meeting, Mrs. Gordons asked me for recommendations on how to resolve this mother-daughter tension. She was desperate for answers. She said, "I love Betty very much and she knows it. But why is she so rebellious? I came to you because I thought you might be able to help."

This mother was a sincere Christian, and her teenage daughter had been a continual object of her prayers. She could not get Betty to study, get along with her brother, do daily chores correctly, or even eat properly. Home life for them had become an ongoing, mother-daughter battle, and Mrs. Gordons said the situation distressed her terribly. "It's been very trying, believe me," she said.

Probing for the cause of the festering trouble, I asked her what feelings surfaced in her when Betty defied her.

She told me that she had been feeling impatient with her daughter, and her anger had turned into resentment. "But in spite of that," she hastened to add, "I love my daughter very much. Don't you think I have proven this by the torture I've been through in keeping to myself the irritation she causes me?"

My response shocked Mrs. Gordons. She may have been expecting me to side with her, but instead I said, "Your bitter feelings toward Betty are not feelings of love."

"How can you say such a thing?" she cried.

I answered her response by opening my Bible to show her God's description of love. One by one we reviewed the fourteen components of love that are listed in 1 Corinthians 13:4–8.

I also explained to her that kindness and longsuffering are two of the fruits of the Holy Spirit that are produced within the surrendered Christian (see Galatians 5:22–25).

I told Mrs. Gordons that hiding her impatience and resentment did not alter the fact that they were present in her heart. "These are not the ingredients of love," I explained. "These are products of your selfish nature. You may pretend to your daughter, Betty—and to yourself—that they do not exist, but they do!" (She had told me so herself.)

Mrs. Gordons was very surprised when I traced the anguish of her heart to the fact that she was acting lovingly rather than being loving.

"Do you mean that Betty should be allowed to get away with what she does?" she demanded.

"Not at all," I answered. "Yes, your daughter's behavior must be dealt with. However, you cannot deal with it effectively until you first deal with your own inner spirit."

Months later, Mrs. Gordons understood that in order for her to truly love Betty, the impatience and resentment would have to be replaced by genuine patience, kindness, and gentleness. "I'm not capable of patience," she exclaimed in desperation one day. "It is so hard to be kind."

It had been easy for me to see that she needed patience, but now she was realizing this herself. I had been waiting for Mrs. Gordons to realize this because I knew that when she saw her need for patience and asked God for it, He would indeed give it to her.

Then the happy day came when Mrs. Gordons finally dropped her defenses and asked God to give her the love she lacked. As He answered the prayers of her heart, she discovered that God gives the measure of overflowing love He is asked to give. The study of the Scriptures, prayer, and pastoral counseling had yielded abundant love and the fruits of the Spirit in Mrs. Gordons's life. Her love for her daughter was now steadfast and unwavering. Mrs. Gordons now understood that, regardless of how her daughter behaved, she could respond in love. By God's mercy, love, and grace, Mrs. Gordons's loving guidance was now consistent, no longer dependent upon her daughter's behavior.

Sadly, all too many people work very hard at acting lovingly, but spend little time in fellowship with "He who is Love." There is a big difference between acting lovingly and being one who loves others. In fact, as I pointed out earlier in this chapter, selfish motives may be at the root of why a person acts lovingly. A person may behave in a loving way because she wants something for herself. However, a person with a loving spirit will be motivated by the love of God that is within her.

I am happy to say that Mrs. Gordons's consistent love also yielded a wonderful change in her daughter's life. In fact, Betty responded so well to her mother's loving spirit that their relationship was restored, and their home is now the splendidly happy, Christian home it should be!

Following God's Example of Unfailing Love

Who sets the tone in a family: the parents or the children? Although she didn't know it, Mrs. Gordons was setting the tone in her home. She thought the tension was her daughter's fault, but she found that the home atmosphere changed when she changed. We often hear parents complain, "I get so tired of kids! They wear me out." Mothers of preschoolers have even said to me, "If my three-year-old would behave, I'd be happy." These women were actually serious when they made these statements. Imagine how unhappy these adults must be if they have resigned themselves to the flimsy idea that their happiness (or lack of it) depends upon the behavior of their preschooler!

This misconception is not just held by parents of very young children. Sadly, many parents of older children also hold to the idea that their own happiness is reliant upon how the children living in their homes are behaving. Sadly, many of these parents have given up on their children and have determined to postpone their own happiness until the day comes when their adolescents or teenagers are finally old enough to move out of the house or go off to college. That is a long time to wait to be happy. This is also a very long time for the tone in a family to be one of hardship.

Parents who think their happiness depends on the behavior of their children will see their roles as drudgery. In a short period of time, the parent will resent the child. The end result may then be that the relationship between parent and child begins to break down. However, a parent's love should never be broken down by the child's behavior.

The fellowship between parent and child may indeed be broken, but the parent's portion of the relationship can be quite whole even when the child has withdrawn from the parent's love. Just as God is not the one who breaks fellowship with His children (of all ages), parents should follow His example and be anxiously awaiting the moment when their children will turn back to their love.

Clearly there are consequences when people turn away from that which is true, right, and acceptable in God's sight, but it is important for us to take into account that His intent is always to yield good and plentiful fruit in our lives. He never withdraws His love from us. In fact, even during times when we are doing something our own way and resisting His way, He is eagerly waiting for us to turn back to Him.

In turn, there are consequences when our children do wrong. Sometimes we must implement direct consequences, and at other times we must stand by while they suffer natural consequences for their poor choices. However, parents who are filled with God's love will respond like He does. When our children separate themselves from our love, we must be like Him: steadfast and unwavering, waiting with open arms for the moment when they will turn their hearts toward us and receive our love and care again. Just as God is waiting for us to confess and turn from our sins, parents' love for their children should remain unwavering during times when their children are rejecting their love.

Always remember God's example of unchanging love: Even while He is allowing us to suffer the consequences of resisting His ways, He is appealing to us constantly: "'Come to Me, all you who labor and are heavy laden, and I will give you rest'" (Matthew 11:28).

Yes, God constantly has our good in mind. Because of His goodness and love, His mercy and grace are always at work in His children's lives. Because He is always mindful of what is best for us, He does not leave us unattended. Even temporary consequences that may seem hard for a season of time are meant for our good. His love, mercy, and grace constantly provide guideposts to keep us from going our own way. By the same token, our love for our children should be constant. It should be consistently guiding them to closely follow the pathway that is true and right.

You Are Not Alone

Most people dream of having a home that is full of peace, love, joy, and tranquility; however, frustration often results when they examine the disparity between what is and what could (or should) be. Many parents feel overwhelmed, frustrated, and even inadequate when they take time to assess their homes and realize they are not happy ones.

Have you been feeling this kind of frustration?

If so, please take comfort in the fact that God does not expect you to do all of this alone. Your heavenly Father is watching over you and your children. Remember, a warm and friendly home is a matter of the Spirit, not a matter of the flesh. No set of procedures or particular parenting style ensures that a home will be a healthy place where all family members and relationships are flourishing. Actually, home management comes in many styles. Some management styles are strict and some are lenient. The parenting and home management style is not what ensures healthy ground in which families grow up in Jesus Christ.

So how do parents meet the ongoing challenges of guiding their children in a way that reflects the image of God? Only by the Spirit of God is this possible.

If we reflect on the fact that God created all of us in His own image, we may begin to grasp the necessity of loving those He has placed in our care. Families are in constant change. Over time, a wide variety of different interests, needs, and capacities will emerge in the individual members of your family. Without His Spirit, the task of being a parent would be truly overwhelming. But you are not alone. By His Spirit, you can rely on Him to make you sensitive to the individual needs of each member of your family. As you pray and seek God's ways, He will give you love for your children. You do not have to pretend to have the fourteen components of love that we noted earlier in this chapter. God is the source of love, so look to Him for the love that you need.

ADULT CONVICTION, CONFIDENT EXPECTATION

Now that we have examined how guiding and disciplining children need to be an outflow of love, we will add another strategic point. Although *adult conviction* and *confident expectation* do not sound like biblical terms, they are important components of effective parenting.

By *confident expectation* I mean that you are doing or requiring something you believe is in the best interest of the child. If you are confidently expecting good results, you will have the conviction that will be necessary to follow through with your plan.

However, for a parent's confident expectation to be valid, two other components must be present:

1. The parent's manner must be friendly, gentle, and firm.
2. The parents must be in agreement with one another.

It is important to keep in mind that in the long run our children generally model our good—and bad—behaviors. Only telling them what they should do is a much less effective, and often ineffective, means of instilling values in our children. To understand this concept better, we can assess how a parent may guide his child to live out one of the Ten Commandments: "'Honor your father and your mother, that your days may be long upon the land which the LORD your God is giving you'" (Exodus 20:12).

Of course, all parents want their children to honor them, but how do we teach this to our children?

Do we want them to just "act like" they are honoring us, or do we want them to really honor us from their hearts? Certainly we want them to honor us from their hearts, but then doesn't that imply that we must first be honorable ourselves and that our children will see, hear, and experience the fruit of that commandment working in and through us?

Of course, being honorable in nature will lead us to do what we are seeking to teach our children to do. If we only tell our children to honor us, how will they understand how to do this? Our children will understand the concept of honoring us when they observe us honoring other people. Seeing that attribute at work in us will not only help them understand the concept and provide them with godly examples to emulate, but also allow them to give honor to us because we are honorable in nature—and not just because of the position we hold in their lives. Exodus 20:12 implies certain conditions:

1. Parents honor their child's grandparents.
2. Each parent of the child honors the other parent of the child—regardless of whether or not the mother and father are married and living in the same household.
3. Parents honor anyone who is in a position of authority.

In other words, the best way to teach your children to honor you is to honor the people with whom you interact.

Whether we realize it or not, we are constantly teaching and modeling behavior in front of our children. This is why good parenting is a matter of whether or not the parent's spirit is surrendered to the Spirit of God, and is not limited to a set of skills and procedures. A parent cannot pretend to be loving or pretend to lead a godly life all day long, day in and day out. At some point the pretense will be uncovered and the real spirit of the parent will be revealed—usually under pressure. Children are watching and listening to their parents and other adults much more than most grown-ups realize. Regardless of whether or not adults understand their degree of influence, children are always watching for behavior to imitate and values to internalize.

Parenting Implies a Purpose and a Goal

Parenting cannot be haphazard. In fact, the very essence of guiding children implies a purpose and a goal. It suggests that parents assume responsibility for influencing their children and for making their learning experiences wholesome and effective.

To be effective teachers who have fair expectations of their children, parents must educate themselves about how and at what rate infants, toddlers, preschoolers, school-age children, preteens, teenagers, and young adults develop. This is important if parents are to have realistic expectations of what a child may normally be able to do during a particular age span. For example, a parent will only set the child up for failure and frustration if he expects a preschooler to perform a task that she will not be developmentally ready to do until she is older. By the same token, a parent may also overreact to his adolescent's moodiness if he does not understand the results of hormonal changes that occur as young girls and boys emerge into young women and men.

Parents should keep in mind that children develop in accordance with their own individual, God-given timetables; however, basic knowledge of child development will enable parents to provide the tools, experiences, and guidance that a child generally needs during a given age span. For example, an infant may need visual, auditory, and tactile stimulation; a toddler will need more opportunities for increasing his physical strength and developing his motor and verbal skills; and the preschooler will need more activities that will help her further develop her cognitive, fine motor, and socialization skills. Parents of school-age children, adolescents, and teens also need to acquire a basic understanding of human development. For example, understanding how children process information and form opinions at different ages enables parents to recognize how to lay the foundation of faith, lead their children to a personal relationship with their Savior, and deepen their relationship with Him. Your desire to learn about your task and your willingness to risk making mistakes will enrich your child's life in ways you had not considered before.

As you study and put into practice your own ideas and some of the procedures that have been successfully used by other adults, you will gradually acquire more and more skill in the art of arranging experiences that foster wholesome and happy development in your children. At first you will develop understanding, and then in time your conviction about your expanding plan will grow.

Why is a parent's conviction about a plan important? It is important because the effectiveness of any procedure coincides with the adult's confidence in the idea that the plan is beneficial to the child. Confidence and conviction will dissipate a parent's fear that opposition from the child will last long or breed hostilities in the child that will harm him later in life.

Parents do not often realize the harm they are causing when they allow their children to have their own way. In some cases, the children are in control of the family situation because the parents have not formulated a specific plan and decided to stick with it. In other cases, the parents have not fully embraced the responsibility of being parents. They may be going through some of the motions of being parents, but are only giving a halfhearted effort, taking shortcuts whenever possible.

A Mother's Bothersome Task becomes a Gift from the Lord

One case comes to mind about a mother who asked me for help because her ten-year-old would not eat during mealtimes. When I asked the mother about her daughter's eating routine, it was quite obvious to me that the girl could not possibly be hungry at dinnertime. How could she be? Every day after school she came home and ate an unlimited supply of sandwiches, cookies, and fruit right up until it was time for the family to sit down together and eat supper. The needed plan of action was clear to me, but the mother seemed surprised when I suggested that she limit her daughter's snacking. In fact, the mother indicated to me that she regarded this as a form of cruelty because she still remembered how she felt when she was a child and her own mother had withheld food from her.

This mother I was counseling had already made a halfhearted effort for a day or two to limit her daughter's snacking, but because she had not been convinced that her plan was good for her child, she did not follow through with helping her daughter to eat nutritious foods and enjoy mealtimes with the family.

Because the daughter's bitter tears had easily convinced the mother to back down from her plan, the child continued to pick at her supper. This was a source of irritation for both parents. The mother was also very annoyed that the child was careless about cleaning her room and doing other chores.

We soon discovered that the root of the problem was actually much deeper than the daughter's eating habits. Over a period of time the mother admitted that she felt parenting was a bothersome task. Furthermore, it was evident that she was not committed to the responsibility of being a good parent because there was no conviction behind the behavioral boundaries she and her husband set and then quickly rescinded for their daughter. These parents had not taken any steps to formulate a plan they both agreed upon. They had not prayed about, researched, meditated upon, and discussed the details related to what was best for their daughter.

When the mother admitted that being a parent was a source of irritation for her, she realized that her irritation with her daughter went much deeper than just how she felt about the girl's eating habits and failure to do chores. She began to see that her own response to her daughter's behavior was also a response to her daughter as a person. When she saw this correlation, she understood that her actions and feelings, and therefore her heart, were falling far short of the "spectrum of love."

As the mother saw her own need, she turned to God for His love. He was faithful to answer her prayers when He turned her dissatisfaction into joy and her self-centeredness into a giving and loving spirit. Step by step, He also unfolded a plan for how she and her husband would guide the child and follow through with their commitments to specific strategies for leading, helping, and teaching their child. The mother's boldness increased as God filled her heart with love for her daughter and for her role as her parent. As her relationship with the Lord grew stronger, she became more and more confident in her expectation that God's blessing was upon her efforts to do what was best for her child. As she gave God charge over her life, the child moved into the structure of family routines and began eating healthily. At first the girl needed strong consequences for resisting her parents' newly defined parameters, but over time she yielded more and more to their congenial, but firm, supervision.

Gradually the mother grew in her understanding of her parental responsibility and accepted it. The mother had once considered parenting a bothersome task. Now her conviction about her God-given responsibility became increasingly steadfast. Her success with her child grew in proportion to her own development.

NONCOMPLIANT BEHAVIOR

You may be wondering:

1. *Why are conviction and confident expectation so necessary?*
   Because without them, the parent will back down from doing what is best for the child. We saw an example of this when the mother backed down from limiting her daughter's snacks.
2. *Why would a parent not do what is best for the child?*
   If a parent is not convinced she is doing what is best for the child, she will be unsure of what to do and will be easily swayed from following through with a plan.

A child's resistance to adult authority is one area that calls upon a parent's resolve. Because every child will test the limits to his freedom of choice, parents should not be surprised when the child resists their guidelines. If you know your child will resist from time to time, you have plenty of time to seek God's wisdom about how to respond to your child when this happens.

In his epistle to the church in Rome, Paul quoted the psalmist, who said, "'There is none righteous, no, not one'" (Romans 3:10). This Scripture implies that all parents will come face-to-face with children's natural tendency to resist authority. We know this by common experience with other parents and because the Scripture tells us that there is not one righteous (innocent or holy) person. A child's resistance to authority will challenge the parent's conviction to her plan and test his confident expectation that her decision will yield good fruit in the child.

But what is resistance? Resistance is a means of control that many children are allowed to use day in and day out. Some carry this spirit into adulthood without having been taught its true nature and the remedy.

In our experience, children are not at ease when they are "getting away with something." You may be surprised by the fact that a child will naturally be aching for boundaries even when he is rebelling against his parents' authority. Although he may be at a new height of rebellion and making it as hard for his parents as possible, he will still be looking for his parents to help him move back into the security and safety of an enforced set of standards. It may outwardly appear like the child is gleeful when he gets away with something, but in truth he will feel unsettled and unsafe. This is because children are bewildered and disturbed when parents indulge lawless behavior in their children. On the other hand, children feel at ease when definite standards are set up. When administered firmly and with kindness, standards that parents place on their children's behavior are safeguards and boundaries in which the children can rest.

What is noncompliance? It is failure to comply. By noncompliant behavior we mean that children are behaving in a way that does not comply with the adult's requests or standards for behavior. Parents who consistently foster noncompliant behavior in their children should not expect good results. Obviously, this is the opposite of what we refer to as a "confident expectation" of good results. It is unlikely that parents would intentionally encourage their children to be noncompliant.

However, many parents do not realize they are allowing their children to manipulate them—and rewarding them for it.

One common form of noncompliance occurs when the child is not required to perform a task he is asked to do. In some households it is common for these power struggles between parent and child to happen many times throughout the course of a day. There are three steps to what we call a "child's avoidance/escape procedure." Here are some examples of possible scenarios:

Request: Time to get up!
Noncompliance: Child doesn't get up.
Outcome: Parent does not require compliance with request and does not administer consequences for noncompliance.

Request: Hang up your clothes.
Noncompliance: Child hangs up one shirt and leaves the rest on the floor.
Outcome: Parent does not require compliance with request and does not administer consequences for noncompliance.

Request: Eat your peas.
Noncompliance: Child hides some peas under the mashed potatoes.
Outcome: Parent does not require compliance with request and does not administer consequences for noncompliance.

Request:	Close the door.
Noncompliance:	Child plops down in front of the television instead.
Outcome:	Parent does not require compliance with request and does not administer consequences for noncompliance.

Request:	Stay seated.
Noncompliance:	Child slouches until he purposefully falls out of his chair.
Outcome:	Parent does not require compliance with request and does not administer consequences for noncompliance.

The longer a child is not required to comply, the more experienced he becomes in manipulating and controlling his parents. Parents only make matters worse when they have emotional outbursts and yet still fail to appropriately and successfully guide the child to complete the task. The parent may threaten, nag, bluster, explode, or even physically assault the child, but these emotionally driven responses often invite the veteran child to make a game out of seeing how long it will take his parents to get distracted or give up on requiring him to comply.

The child, who has not succeeded in easily sneaking his way out of doing what his parents have requested, has other means of maintaining his position of noncompliance. These strategies may include whining, crying, yelling, sulking, and displaying tantrums. Older children may accuse their parents of not loving them or of being unfair. Teenagers may even try to physically intimidate their parents.

The games will continue day in and day out if the parents are not fully invested in having God at the center of their personal and family life; if they are not focused on fulfilling parental responsibilities as unto the Lord; and if they are not wholly committed to doing what is best for the child. Parents may have good intentions and yet still be controlled by the child's manipulative games. As long as parents cannot recognize manipulative behavior, they will become confused by it and give in to it. However, as parents grow in their *confident expectation* that their plan will yield good results and as they become more *committed* to expand and follow through with their plan, they will more easily recognize and refuse to be dissuaded by any manipulative tactics their children may try to use on them.

Noncompliant behavior has predictable consequences:

1. *It hinders peer group relations.* Children who do not cooperate with adults usually have not developed the social skills necessary for them to cooperate with other children. Rather than asking for a toy, the older preschool child may grab it from another child. The adolescent girl may be unable to maintain lasting friendships because she gossips and is untrustworthy. The teenage boy may not understand why his classmates think he is irritating.

2. *It hinders progress in school.* Being out of one's seat, disrupting the class, and resisting study time results in lower grades and failure to acquire study skills.

3. *It leads to antisocial behavior.* As these children grow older and continue socializing with other children, noncompliance is acted out in various forms of aggressive, dishonest, and manipulative behaviors that do not recognize the rights of others. Also, the other children who typically cooperate with each other will reject the child who consistently fails to behave in socially accepted ways.

4. *It leads to low self-esteem.* It is lonely being a rebel. When a child sees herself as less than adequate, she may begin to have difficulty receiving and giving love. She will then gravitate to other children who often exhibit noncompliant behavior. Her attempts to impress her new peers will only make matters worse.

Clearly, helping a child to comply is a necessary and fundamental part of being a parent. The best way to teach compliance is to demonstrate it: to rein in your own inert impulses, guard your language, and do the right thing at the right time. I believe that the constant scrutiny of your own kids must be the toughest tests of character and spiritual stamina yet devised.

TAKE YOUR CHILD'S HEALTH INTO CONSIDERATION

- Is your child not eating because she has health problems or is anorexic or is bulimic?
- Is your child unable to complete a task because she has a learning disability or is somehow physically impaired?
- Is your child not paying attention in school because she is worried about an illness in the family?
- Is your teenager withdrawing from you because he is on drugs?
- Is your daughter avoiding you because she is sexually active and afraid you will find out?

Do not be quick to assume that your child's behavior is as simple as noncompliance. Know your child, foster open and honest communication within your family, study up on the signs of health problems, and educate yourself about the behaviors that signal an older child is in trouble.

Do your homework and diligently seek wisdom from God, godly counsel, and medical help whenever you suspect your child needs extra help!

God's unfailing love working in and through you is clearly exhibited when you take all measures necessary for providing superior care for the children He has entrusted to you.

Throughout this chapter we have emphasized how important it is for your children to know that your love for them is steadfast. We have also examined how essential it is for you to be confidently expecting that your efforts will help them succeed, stay healthy, feel safe, receive and give love, and develop an increasingly close relationship with the Lord. We have also stressed that your children will know that you mean what you say when your confident expectation leads to a strong conviction to develop, expand, and fulfill the parenting plan that you and your partner have agreed upon.

FAMILY DEVOTIONS

This leads us to a primary component of a happy and healthy home where loving spirits are nourished in His love: family devotions.

We often hear that "family devotions" are the key to family success. This period of time when the family regularly pauses to worship and learn of the Lord together should be at the center of every family's spiritual health plan. Compelling the family to regularly gather together for times of devotion to the Lord requires discipline. However, it will be easier to stay committed to making it a routine part of family life if parents present it to the children as a special time together and a necessity for maintaining a healthy family unit.

Devotions can be a time of true "togetherness" when family members share questions, doubts, thoughts, problems, and answers. Hearing one another pray or learning verses of Scripture together regularly establishes and reinforces the fact that God is at the center of the family unit. Helping children apply the teaching of the Word to their school subjects makes learning easier and more fun, and helps the children more clearly identify how the Word of God is the center of daily life and not just reserved for special times spent in church or devotions. Encouraging each family member to testify—to tell others about what the Lord has recently revealed to them or how He has helped them in their daily lives—will pave the way for more discussion about spiritual matters at other times.

Despite the obvious benefits, many parents over the years have told me that maintaining family devotions has been a difficult task for them. Apparently, because their children sometimes resist participating, parents are forever looking for some book or other aid that will help them make the gatherings more attractive to and interesting for the children. Then, because the new material does not alleviate the children's resistance, the parents quickly give in to the children's noncompliant behavior.

In my opinion, the success of family devotions relies much more on the parents' conviction to have them than it does on a specific technique or carefully chosen material. Parents must first ask themselves: Is having family devotions vital to the welfare of my children?

To gain some perspective, let's compare and contrast family devotions with activities that are typically high priorities in most households. For example, why would requiring your child to participate in family devotions be less of a priority than making sure he brushes his teeth, washes his hands, wears clean clothes, or maintains his best efforts in school.

When you think about it, you will probably see that it is quite a normal occurrence for you to see that your child does other things you consider necessary for his well-being. For instance, when supper is ready, you round up the family regardless of whether they are absorbed in doing something else. There is no question about your adolescent going to school on days when he would rather go surfing, snowboarding, or shopping at the mall. If your teenager has trouble with her studies, it never occurs to you to let her stay home from classes for a few days so she can rest up and watch some television. You take your preschooler to the doctor or dentist even if he screams and you have to hold him close to you until he feels safe enough to stay calm on his own. You make sure your school-age child wears her coat when it is cool outside—even if she thinks wearing a coat makes her look "uncool."

If you insist on adherence to what you say on so many other matters you consider to be in the best interest of your children, then why would you not also insist that they participate in family devotions? The fact of the matter is this: If you truly consider family devotions vital to you and to your children's welfare, you will make sure it becomes an integral part of your household routine. You will overlook resistance to it like you do in other matters. Then when your children see your unyielding commitment to having family devotions in which all family members participate, they will soon realize that their resistance will be of no avail. And you can be sure that before long, they will start looking forward to your undivided time together.

The success of using devotional books or other materials will rely on your *confident expectation* and *commitment*. Your certainty that family devotions are vitally important to you and your family is what will make the difference. Your confident expectation of vital results will lead to the commitment that will be necessary for you to sidestep the distractions, divert and silence the excuses, and fulfill what you have committed yourself and your family to consistently do.

If the benefits of the family devotions are reflected in your daily life and in your relationships with your children, your spouse, and other people, you can be sure that your child will hold fast to keeping devotion to God at the center of their lives and that they will impart this expression of love to their children and to their children's children.

7

DISCIPLINE
INVOLVES SETTING
LIMITS

THOUGHT STARTER

Limits provide security for children and their parents.

MEMORY VERSE

"You shall set bounds for the people all around."

EXODUS 19:12

IF YOU HAVE THE RESPONSIBILITY OF GETTING SOMETHING done in the family, then setting the limits will be required. Determining the limits is the first step; the next step is helping your children observe those limits. What limits the children want to keep is not the question. The question is, What do you believe is in the best interests of your children? What are reasonable limits that must be observed? They should be reasonable according to your judgment and not according to theirs. The Lord told Moses, "'You shall set bounds for the people all around'" (Exodus 19:12).

THE PERFECT PLAY

A football stadium in my home state seats 100,000 people. Every fall it is repeatedly filled by people who fight traffic jams, are jostled by crushing crowds, and suffer through rain, sleet, and snow for several hours.

What magnetizes these fans to brave these conditions, while at the same time drawing other fans to gather friends and neighbors around their television sets? It is the pleasure and satisfaction that comes from watching eleven men cooperate as one unit to produce—in a sudden, dramatic moment—a long run, a beautiful pass, or a touchdown!

I have been in the University of Michigan stadium when all the fans suddenly leaped to their feet at the same time and cheered. What could possibly happen that would cause 100,000 people to do the same thing at the same time? The perfect play!

To pull off the perfect play, a player must be willing to subject his own will to a common cause. When it is done right, the perfect play is a beautiful, magical thing to watch. What makes the perfect play possible is everyone being subjected to one plan and everyone working together—whether it was his idea or not. Each man has his job and can use any legal technique he desires that is within the parameters of the team's plan for that play. Every man is doing his job...and with flair. That is what creates the perfect play; it is beautiful to watch.

But notice that flair is not enough. Every man doing his own thing with flair does not make the perfect play. Everyone has to be working together.

There are some other features about the game that draw people.

1. The size and shape of the playing fields are always the same.
2. The way the game is played is always governed by the same set of rules.
3. The boundaries that limit the playing area are always the same.

4. The players' uniforms are always the same because the school colors do not change.
5. The players are determined and obligated to cooperate with each other, under the watchful guidance of a coach.

REFEREEING

In a football game, the home and visiting teams, and their corresponding fans all go by the same rules and boundaries. These rules are published in a book, and knowledge of these rules is essential to understanding the game.

Making sure the players stay within the limits established by the rule book is the job of the officials. If a player breaks a rule, the referee penalizes the entire team. The player and his team must accept the consequences.

This is no big deal. The team simply accepts their consequences and the game goes on. If a player or coach protests the official's decision too much and gets kicked out of the game, the crowd may approve of the protest. However, the referee's interpretation of the game is final. He who argues with the official gets kicked out of the game, but not off the team: Remember, *he is kicked out of the game, but not off the team.*

YOUR LIMITS MAKE YOU UNIQUE

The phrase *football game* tells us many things. The very name of the game determines the shape of the ball, the dimensions of the playing field, the rules of the game, and the type of clothes the players and officials wear.

The word *family* also tells us many things. Determined limits make a family unique. A list of identifying marks of, say, the Landrum family may look something like this:

- address
- type of house
- church
- school
- style of recreation
- mealtime
- table manners
- television time
- how they dress
- house rules
- choice of toys
- neatness
- contact with friends
- entertaining at home

A closer look at the Landrum family allows us to observe some specific limits.

1. They eat a balanced meal.
2. They don't eat crackers or other such food on the living room couch.
3. The children pick up their toys when they are through with them.
4. They hang up their clothes.
5. The family sits together at church.
6. Each child has a regular bedtime.

Do these limits sound reasonable? Many others would make up the sometimes written, but usually unwritten, list of limits for a particular household. Our list here is only a sample. In fact, every family's set of limits is unique, but certain components are common to most because they are based on common sense. Some limits are fully established and do not change over the course of time, while others will naturally evolve as the children grow and mature. Infants usually experience their first limits when they try to squirm out of their car seat or stroller. It is also a major discovery when babies crawl right into the baby gate that divides them from a set of stairs. Young preschoolers usually learn the basic limits that will take many forms throughout their whole lifetimes. These include limits pertaining to health and safety, respecting property, and respecting other people's rights and feelings.

Remember, limits provide a basis for consistency and structure that ensure the well-being of your children. If you are consistent, your children will know what to expect. When limits are consistent, they are more easily internalized by the children, and following them becomes a lifestyle for them. This will help them become adults who have self-control and who easily conform to the limits of society.

Limits alone will not eliminate the problem of human nature—the sinfulness of your children. Limits will not change children's basic attitudes, or their spirits. In fact, limits will often reveal attitude and spirit.

By setting limits

1. you allow your children some freedom of choice;
2. you make things a little more predictable;
3. you provide a framework for dealing with your children.

DISCIPLINE INVOLVES HELP

Children will never maintain limits perfectly. They will need lots of reminders, particularly when they are in new situations that require new limits. We must also keep in mind that children have their ups and downs just like adults do, and some days they will need more help than others. We saw a good example of this in our last chapter when we saw how Terry arrived at the daycare tired and cranky, and within minutes of stepping out onto the playground, he bit his friend who got to the tricycle before he did.

Terry needed extra help that day even though he knew exactly what the rule was about biting. Because he did not try to negotiate with Jose, we can assume that Terry did not understand the concept of sharing. A savvy five-year-old probably would have had some pretty appealing ideas up his sleeve with which to negotiate.

The idea of young preschoolers struggling to grasp the idea of sharing toys is something that challenges every parent and caregiver. This brings to mind the experience of another preschool teacher that clearly shows how confusing it can be for a child when he is presented with a concept he is not able to comprehend.

One afternoon, Mrs. White attempted to show Johnny how to share toys with the other children in his preschool class. She thought the three-year-old boy may have understood what she was saying, but it was not long before she discovered that this was certainly not the case. At first she was quite pleased when she saw that Fajai was playing with a little car and Johnny was curiously watching him. But then, much to the teacher's surprise and also to Fajai's, Johnny suddenly slipped up behind Fajai, grabbed the car out of Fajai's hand, and said, "Let's share." Obviously, Johnny had misunderstood what his teacher had attempted to teach him!

Did Johnny need to be scolded? Certainly not! Obviously, he had not yet developed the cognitive skills necessary for understanding the concept of sharing. It may be safe to assume that prior to learning about this great idea called *sharing,* he knew that grabbing toys was not the way you do things at preschool. And just a few minutes earlier, "Teacher" had told him that grabbing toys from your friends was a good thing as long as he called it *sharing!* Now it was time to celebrate his new discovery and "share" with Fajai.

Ah, but life returned to normal when the teacher told him in a very gentle and firm manner, "You must give it back.... When Fajai is finished playing with the car, you may play with it."

Of course, Johnny did not want to give the car back. He was probably completely confused because the teacher seemed to be saying something different from what she had said a few minutes ago. Life at preschool can sure be confusing at times.

Well, life was obviously back to normal, and so Johnny begrudgingly gave the car back to Fajai—with a lot of help from the teacher. Johnny realized he would have to settle for playing with blocks now.

Teacher had a way of making blocks seem like a lot of fun when she was trying to get a kid not to want a car anymore. Hey, she even sat down to play with blocks too. That was better than playing with a little old car anyway. Johnny probably thought to himself, *Hmm, Fajai is over here playing with blocks now because he saw Teacher over here with me. That car doesn't look so great sitting there in the middle of the floor with nobody else playing with it. I think I'll just play with blocks. Teacher says maybe I should give this cool-looking block to Fajai because it would look great on his castle. Hmm, well, maybe…not this time.*

The adult's choice of how to deal with what appears to be noncompliance must always take into consideration a child's developmental readiness for a specific idea or activity. For example, Mrs. White had to take the toy away from Johnny, but his resistance to giving the toy up was related to his confusion. Rather than scolding him, she redirected him to another activity and then gave him a little nudge in the direction of sharing when she suggested that he might want to let Fajai use the block. By doing this, she was hinting at what the concept of sharing really means. She was obviously being mindful of the fact that young three-year-olds are usually not developmentally ready to learn how to share.

Until they are very close to age four, most preschoolers are only ready for parallel play, where they play next to one another. Generally speaking, young three-year-olds do not cooperate well together when they are using the same materials. For example, gently introducing the child to the concept of sharing is fine, but he may be much happier sitting next to his friend while they each play with separate toys. But one day, Johnny will probably say to Fajai, "Hey, let's trade toys for a while."

HELP IN APPLYING THE RULE

Depending on the age of the child, you may give the simple rule with or without the reason. Very young children think concretely and will not be able to grasp the reasons for the limit unless you can explain it in four simple words or less. Even then, he might not make the connection. The older child, on the other hand, will want to know the reason. Telling the child the reason has the benefit of helping the child develop reasoning skills. However, you do not need to repeat that reason twenty times over. If the older child is asking you to explain yourself over and over, he is probably looking for a means of escaping conformity.

In either case, children often need a little help applying the rule. Sometimes children will not understand what you were saying. Other times they understand quite well but will test you to see if you really mean what you say. And still other times, children need help understanding to what situations the rule applies.

It is important to note that children learn best by doing. An older child will remember 90 percent of what he hears *and* sees *and* touches, but he will only learn 10 percent of what he hears the first time. The younger a child is, the more he will rely on learning through doing. This is because he will not have the language skills required for learning very much through verbal communication, and he often will not have the cognitive skills he needs for correctly interpreting what he sees. A good example of this is that Mrs. White was not very effective when she tried to teach Johnny by explaining to him what *sharing* means. However, when she sat on the floor with him and suggested that he might want to let Fajai use his block, Mrs. White was using a language he understood and experiences that were familiar to him.

Older children and adults have their own learning styles. Some of us learn best by seeing something related to the material; others learn best when they write down or do something else related to the material; and others learn best when they hear the information. It would be very helpful to you and your children if you would consider their learning styles when you present information to them. For example, you may tell your teenagers, Tyler and Tina, that you want the house cleaned by the time you get home. Tyler may be an auditory learner so he heard and absorbed every word you said, while Tina, on the other hand, may be paying more attention to what you are wearing and wondering if you still have a headache. Of course, it wouldn't really be fair to punish Tina if you knew very well that she is a visual learner and is only able to absorb less than 10 percent of what she hears for the first time. To give both children the best possible chance at success, you would want to tell them your request and write it down—or make sure that Tina writes your instructions down while you are standing there. Of course, only leaving a list for Tyler may not be effective if he is an auditory learner and does not even notice notepads the size of wallpaper.

The point here is that parents are teachers. Have you ever been completely frustrated with your eight-year-old because her bed is always made sloppily, only to discover you never showed her how to make her bed? Or have you ever told a preschooler to clean his room and fifteen minutes later you find him sitting on the floor playing with the blocks he is supposed to be putting away. But then when you are about ready to scold him for not cleaning his room, he beams up at you, proud of himself because he threw all of his clean clothes in the dirty clothes basket. The importance of knowing your child's developmental level, learning style, and level of knowledge about the task at hand cannot be stressed enough.

You must work with your children in the spirit of a helpful teacher. Remember that children learn day by day as they are developmentally ready to move on to the next step. Everything should not be taught in one day, and parents must be careful not to assume that their children know more than they do. Before dishing out consequences, first find out if you did your job of giving your child the best possible opportunity for fulfilling your request. And if your child is unable to do what you have asked, either help him complete the task or modify it in a way that ensures the child can return to you with a smile on his face, knowing that he has done the job well. You have many years to help your children become all God has called them to be. This necessitates understanding and consistency, gentleness and fairness.

THE GAME

So, now it is time to set limits for the family. Think of it: The wonderful opportunity for planning the finest possible life for your children has been set before you. Doesn't that sound like fun? What could be more enjoyable than deciding what is best for the children?

LIMITS: A FIELD TO PLAY ON

In our family, we looked at limits as being areas of freedom…of choice of activities. For example, we had designated certain areas for play. In the living room, you could read or play the stereo.

In the family room, you could play with remote control cars, toys, or games. The only limitation was to put the game or toy back when you were through with it.

There were even some things you could do in the kitchen. You could always help with the dishes. You could help scrape a carrot, peel potatoes, or bake cookies. Mom made all these tasks fun. Or you could sit at the table and talk to her.

Then there was the basement. You had many choices down there: a swing that was screwed to the rafters, a tricycle, and a wagon. There was also a bench—complete with a hammer and nails and a saw. Wood was cut to size so you could nail pieces together. But the real attraction was a piano box that on any given day could serve as a skyscraper or a submarine or a house or whatever prop the children's dramatic play for the day called for.

Outside there was a swing set, which had a swing, parallel bars, and rings. There was another wagon there. And a sandbox…full of toys.

In all these activity areas, the only limitations were that you (1) did not throw things or (2) hit anyone. You had to take your turn. You could make all the noise you wanted in all of these areas except the living room and the family room. These were conversation rooms.

The limits defined the options. The children learned to make choices within the limits and to respect the rights of others.

A FRAMEWORK FOR
DEALING WITH YOUR CHILD

Tony discovered a framework for dealing with Caleb after going out of his way to set what he thought was a reasonable limit with his eleven-year-old. He even got his son Caleb to participate in making the decision.

"Let's set a reasonable limit, Son. Before supper, you wash your hands."

Caleb agreed. "Yes, Dad, that's reasonable."

Of course it was reasonable until just before supper. Then Caleb suddenly disagreed with Dad.

After all, his hands were not *that* dirty, *and* he was hungry and ready for supper. When a rule is new, children need help remembering the limit. However, when they refuse to follow the rule, they will need "extra help." When this happens, the child is probably trying to determine if you mean what you say. In this case, Caleb may have wondered if he could recant his earlier statements about this decision. We can see from this example that children who participate in a decision must realize that once the decision has been made, discussion time is over, and it is time to begin adhering to the limit.

The degree of a child's resistance usually determines the kind and the degree of help that is necessary. When the child has firmly established in his mind that you mean what you say and there will be consequences if he does not comply, abiding by the limit will become part of his routine.

If the limit involves something like washing his hands before meals, parents will need to continue checking to see if this is being done. However, the goal here is to have the child wash his hands before meals for the rest of his life. The establishment of this practice will help ensure present and future health benefits for the child. Of course, Mom and Dad should be washing their hands before meals too. If not, the child will not seriously consider the correlation between washing his hands and maintaining good health. Modeling good hygiene is the best way to establish these healthful habits in our children.

Other limits will be important to children's health. For example, not allowing the child to get enough rest is not a way of helping the child. Even though you may want to spend more time with your child or allow him to watch a special television program on a school night, you must really base your decision on what is best for the health of the child. Parents who work late—and desire to spend more time with their children—often allow their children to stay up too late. Remember, children need a lot more rest than adults do. In fact, young children and adolescents need ten to twelve hours of sleep each night.

Therefore, once you have determined what time is bedtime, it is best to be inflexible, especially on school nights. Also keep in mind that if children are allowed to stay up very late on weekends, their sleep schedules will be disrupted, and they will not be able to get to sleep at bedtime during the week. Children's sleep schedules should not be like a roller coaster. Bedtime should be bedtime. And not time for: "Oh, just this one more TV program." Lack of consistency on this will generally invite the child to resist you during the nights to come because your actions will have shown that you do not really mean what you say.

Along with this, I encourage parents to consider whether watching television right up until the children's bedtime is really a good practice. Being glued to television programming does not facilitate communication between parents and the children. You may want to consider turning off the television altogether and having a time of sharing, storytelling, Bible reading, and praying together. This will be an indirect signal to children that spending time with them and with the Lord is a much higher priority than any television program could possibly be. This also fills them with thoughts of Jesus as they drift off to sleep knowing that you have just wrapped them in the blanket of the Lord's tender arms.

Remember the magnet I mentioned earlier that draws people into the football stadium. It is the thrill and satisfaction of watching eleven men cooperate to produce a sudden and dramatic run, a beautiful pass, or the perfect touchdown play.

Parenthood is like that. Its fascination comes in working together to pull off a pleasant meal, an evening marked by the cheery laughter of happy children, and spending time together in the sweet presence of the Lord before you tuck the children into bed.

The perfect play does not always happen, but keep trying, cooperating, working together, and putting God at the center of everything you do—and you will flourish together in His abundant love.

CHILDREN ARE PEOPLE TOO!

You may be wondering, *What about children's attitudes?* Will limits ruin them emotionally? Remember, guiding children is not changing their spirits. Changing their spirits can only happen when they are born again by the Spirit of God. After this happens, they will become more like Him each day as they sow the Word into their spirits and spend time with Him. Their joy will come from God, just as yours does.

They are people, just like you, but remember that people have turned to their own way and practice evil (see Isaiah 53:6; Romans 7:19). Your children need a Savior too. They have the same drives as you do. That is why their Christian education is important. That is why parenting is a twenty-year process.

I did not think too much about it the evening my daughter approached me just as I was ready to walk up on the platform to speak.

"Hey, Dad, could I have the keys to the car? After the meeting I want to take a carload of kids up to Santa Cruz."

"Okay," I said, without thinking.

Then I went to the platform to make my speech about how important it is for a man and his wife to agree on and be committed to the limits they establish for their children. After I finished my speech, I went to a large foyer in the back of the auditorium where hundreds of people were milling around.

My daughter had a large group of her friends standing behind her when she came up to me and said, "Dad, I want the keys now."

My wife was obviously disturbed when she heard my daughter say this to me. In response to my daughter's announcement that she was ready for the car keys, my wife said to her, "I told you that you couldn't go."

Well, there were some people standing around who heard this exchange; and they started assembling another little congregation to see how the speaker would handle this.

You cannot think of everything, especially when you are traveling. You can expect your children to pick times like that to test the limits. But we had a limit at our house: The first parent you have asked about something gives the last and final answer. Because the limit was clear and consistently kept, my decision was easy. My answer would be easily determined by my daughter's answer to one simple question: Who did you ask about this first—me or your mother?

It turned out she had asked her mother first.

So I said to my daughter, "You know the answer. You asked your mother first."

Her response was, "But, Dad, you are embarrassing me in front of all these people."

Here she not only had willfully tried to disobey her mother by getting permission from me to do something her mother had already told her she could not do, but now was trying to manipulate me by trying to make me feel guilty about embarrassing her in front of all these people.

I want to point out that holding to limits like this one provided security and stability for all of us. I could look to the limit and easily know how to respond; my wife knew that I supported her decisions; and my daughter knew that she could rely on us to be consistent. In that moment, my daughter and wife saw that I was trustworthy.

TONY LEARNS HOW TO BREAK A PROMISE

The need for commitment to the family plan could easily be seen when the Drew family came to me for family counseling. Tony's parents brought their boy to see me because he was smoking and could not be trusted. The parents were concerned about it, and they made a deal with him.

"If you promise to quit smoking, we will buy you a bicycle."

"It's a deal."

So they bought him a bicycle, but it was not long before they realized he was smoking again.

"If you will quit smoking," they said, "we will send you to your favorite summer camp."

"It's a deal"—again without hesitation. When he came home from summer camp they discovered he was smoking again. At this point they brought him to me because they were concerned that they had a son who would not keep his word. They did not trust him.

I had a talk with the boy, and this is what I found out. His father had an idea that you should not have ice cream during the day.

However, Tony's mom would take the kids out for an ice cream sundae after she picked them up from school. The only stipulation was not to tell Dad.

There was something else the boy told me. These people went to a church where one of the standards you accepted when you joined the church was that you would not drink alcoholic beverages. Dad liked a good, cold beer when he came home from work, but he got everyone to promise that "mum's the word" when it came to his beer.

Where did this young fellow get the idea about making an agreement and then breaking it? It is obvious he learned it from his father and mother. These people pretended they were accepting certain limits and then went ahead and broke them. Why shouldn't the boy make a little deal with his dad without intending to keep it? Where did he get the idea? The example for his values and mode of conduct came straight from his father and mother.

When you set a limit, it must be binding on everybody in the family. As mentioned earlier in this book, children much more readily learn values they see at work in their parents. Our actions must match the values we hope and pray will be exhibited in them. If we tell lies in front of our children, they will think lying is okay "under special circumstances." For example, it is much better for your child to see you return that notebook to work that accidentally ended up in your briefcase. If instead you give it to your child to take to school so that you can save a few extra pennies on school supplies, you are telling your child that a little stealing is just fine.

DEFINITION OF FREEDOM

There will be times when you will think a limit is quite sensible, but your children may think it inhibits their freedom too much. Remember, you are the leaders, not your children.

Just what is freedom, anyway? I like this definition: Freedom is the length of a leash from a chosen stake. Picture that. The leash can be short or long. It can be adjusted. There is a lot of freedom between the stake and the outer boundary. When it comes to children, you can give them more or less freedom, depending on how they handle it. Freedom can be adjusted.

I once was driving on a highway in Texas, and my companion said to me, "You are now on the biggest ranch in the entire world." It was so big that the highway we were traveling along ran through the ranch, like a big driveway. Along the road were fences to keep livestock in. There were many cows behind those fences, and they had incredible freedom. Why, you could not even see the other fences that kept them on this ranch. The fences were so far away that they were over the horizon.

Now that was a lot of freedom for those cows! Yet, wouldn't you know, one cow was straining her neck through the fence to get a blade of grass on the other side. The cow had acres to choose from but still opted for trying to stretch her mouth to a few extra inches of ground that were not within her reach.

I thought, *This is just how people behave.* No matter how broad the limits, your children will test them.

As we saw in the example of how our daughter tried to play my wife and me against each other, parents must agree on the limits and support the decisions of the other parent who decides how the limit is to be applied. Without a united front, children learn to play one parent against the other. Another example of this occurred during a church banquet one evening. The situation was similar to the one that happened when our daughter tried to take the car to the beach. The parents were busy socializing at church and did not notice their son's strategy.

Jimmy whispered to his mother, "Can I go to the car and play the radio?"

"No, you may not!" she replied.

So Jimmy watched until his mother was engaged in conversation. He then quietly turned to his father and said, "How about the keys to the car, Dad, so I can go out and listen to the radio?" Without thinking, Dad reached in his pocket, gave his son the keys, and Jimmy disappeared outside. When Dad and Mom came to themselves and realized what had happened, they had to admit that they were not thinking alike and had not been paying attention to what was happening in that particular situation. In situations where you and your partner know that you will both be very distracted from supervising the children, it may be best to designate one particular parent to give special attention to the children's needs and questions.

LIMITS AND NEIGHBORS

Sometimes your children will not be the only ones who disagree with the fairness of your limits. Sometimes neighbors and extended family members may express their opinions about how they think you should be raising your children. When this happens, keep in mind that you have much more experience in life than your children, and you know your children much better than anyone else. Also, you are the ones who have been seeking the Lord for His wisdom.

A very interesting dynamic occurred when the children in a neighborhood all asked their parents if they could cross the highway on their bikes. One of these parents told her son that she did not want him crossing the busy highway on his bicycle. The other parents in the neighborhood said to their children, "If the rest of the mothers say their children can do it, you can do it."

The gang would go to this mother's house and plead for her to let her son cross the highway, but each time she would say, "No! You can't do it."

Her child was distraught about all of this pressure his friends were putting on him, so he begged his mom. "Everybody else's mother says we can go. You always keep us from going."

After this happened a few times, the children asked their moms if they would ignore what this one mom said and let them go anyway. Again, the other mothers said they could only go if all of the other mothers said it was okay. Finally, the harassed mother yielded to the pressure and let them go. Suddenly the children hailed her as being a good mother because she had let them have their way. The children had hardly gotten started when the telephone rang. One of the neighbors called, saying, "Did you tell the children they could cross the street?"

Surprised by her neighbor's tone of voice, the mother said, "Why, yes."

The neighbor replied, "We were depending on you not to let your child go."

It is easy to see that compromising her standard and yielding to pressure had gotten her nowhere. Evidently, the other mothers were not confident enough to stand up to their children themselves and were counting on this mother to hold the line for all of them. They probably assumed she would set the limit for the whole neighborhood because she had done so in the past.

You will never accomplish anything by yielding to this kind of pressure. Like this woman, you may be surprised to find that the very people who seem to oppose you actually silently respect you. And even if they don't agree with you, it should not sway you. Your decisions must be based on what you have decided is best for your child. Your child could be put in harm's way if your decisions are based on what is right in your child's eyes or perhaps in the eyes of the mother next door. And when your child sees you being pleasant to your neighbor, he will learn another valuable lesson: how to respond to people who do not agree with him. If your child sees your resolve coupled with humility and kindness when you respond to your neighbors who do not agree with your decisions, he will see a living example of how biblical principles are applied to daily living.

LIMITS OUTSIDE THE HOME

What your child is learning at home will be expressed in his relationships outside the home. Children are often surprised when they find the approaches they use at home to get their way do not work for them outside their home environment.

Emily had quite a surprise when she started going to preschool. This four-year-old girl was the only child in the family, so she had always been the center of her parents' attention. Of course, she was their pride and joy. And she had learned her manners well: Whenever she wanted something, she would say, "Please, may I have it?" Every time she would do this, her parents' faces would be gleaming because they just couldn't get over how cute she was when she said this. As a reward for being so adorable and polite, Emily was almost always granted her request. And so life went pretty much Emily's way at home.

The first day Emily attended preschool, however, she immediately discovered that things were going to be a little different there. She walked up to a little girl nearby and said, "Please, may I have that doll?" "No," was the answer. Emily returned to her mother with a puzzled look on her face and explained, "I said 'please,' and she won't give it to me."

The mother looked puzzled too. Remember, Emily is this mother's first child, and she thinks the world revolves around her little girl. The teacher had to give both mother and daughter a wake-up call that morning. She told them that certain approaches that had worked well for Emily in the home would not necessarily work well for her outside the home. The wake-up call here was that the other child had rights too. She had the right to decide whether or not she would give Emily the doll, regardless of whether or not she said *please*. Even at a young age, children need opportunities to develop their socialization skills. Emily needed to learn the facts of life, four-year-old style.

ADULTS HAVE LIMITS TOO!

The following excerpts are from a letter a father wrote to his son at the time of his graduation. Though written as humor, it conveys a vital message:

Dear Son,

I'm sure you are thrilled by the idea of taking your place at last in adult affairs—a station of life you probably look upon as a time when "big people" will stop telling you to do things…or not to do things…. Your dad has found out that the chains of adult life are wrought of stiffer stuff than the feeble fetters of childhood. Believe me, no one ever suffered a furrowed brow from such simple commands as "Eat your cereal"…"Do your homework"…"Report for band practice." What once may have seemed a terribly harsh order, "Put away your comic book," will pale into insignificance when compared with "Cut out all pastries and sweets."

The bigger you get, the bigger other people seem to get— if not bigger in stature, then bigger in authority. For example, did you see the look on Dad's face when the Internal Revenue man ordered him to report to the collector's office with all of his…tax receipts?… When a traffic officer says, "Pull over to the curb," Dad pulls over. When Grandmother says, "Roll up the window," Dad rolls up the window. I just want to prepare you for a lifetime of saying, "Yes, sir" to master sergeants, shop foremen, loan company executives, bank tellers, tradesmen, public officials, car dealers, game wardens, and a host of other people you never dreamed were your superiors. Even the most politely phrased commands, like "Please remit" or "Kindly step back in the bus," are still commands. Ushers will order you down an aisle; headwaiters will tell you where to sit; courts will summon you for jury duty; the city hall will notify you to shovel the snow off your sidewalk.

You will be dragged off to parties at other people's houses, and dragged out of bed by people who come to your house. You will be kept off the grass by policemen and kept up by weekend guests…. This is the true life beyond commencement. Congratulations and good luck.

Dad

P.S. Get a haircut for graduation.

LIMITS SHOULD HAVE THE FOLLOWING CHARACTERISTICS:

- They should help a child know what is expected of him.
- They should be reachable, reasonable, and clearly understood.
- They must allow for some freedom of choice.
- There should be as few of them as possible.

In this chapter we have continued our discussion of how instituting structures and boundaries for family members is a fundamental way in which parents can express their love for their children. We have also expanded that idea and pointed out that disciplining our children also includes disciplining ourselves. Our actions need to match our words, and our actions and our words need to be a living expression of the Word of God. The commandments of His Word and the guidance of the Holy Spirit to keep us in His boundaries is an expression of God's love, care, and concern for us. Our external conduct will always be an expression of the time we have (or have not) spent at the feet of our Lord.

8

DISCIPLINE
INVOLVES
HELP

THOUGHT STARTER

You may have to help your child obey.

MEMORY VERSE

And a servant of the Lord must not quarrel but be gentle to all, able to teach, patient, in humility correcting those who are in opposition, if God perhaps will grant them repentance, so that they may know the truth.

2 TIMOTHY 2:24–25

A LIFEGUARD MAY BE SITTING COMFORTABLY UP IN HIS lifeguard chair, tanning himself. If a swimmer suddenly needs his help, the lifeguard who is dedicated to his responsibility for saving lives will not consider these cries to be an interruption. Instead, these swimmers are his primary responsibility.

By the same token, parents need to consider children as their primary responsibility, not as interruptions. "But wait a minute," you say. "Parents have needs too, don't they? They need time to fulfill their personal needs, don't they?" Of course they do. So do waitresses, lifeguards, businessmen, coaches, athletes, secretaries, teachers, and everyone else.

Taking responsibility for leading others is an important part of personal fulfillment. This is true because the joy of giving is closely linked to the joy of living. Sure, being a parent takes a lot of energy. Interacting with children all day long is tiring. There are good days and there are bad days. There are easy days and there are tough days. One day the kids are happy, and another day it seems like they are all grumpy.

Being a parent is a little like being a referee. He keeps the game going smoothly. He is expected to call the plays according to the limits, to be impartial, consistent, and coolheaded. His job can be tough or easy on any given day, depending on the mood of the players, their skill, the importance of the game, and even the weather. Some days, there are few close calls and few penalties. Other days, there can be some debatable, close calls and many penalties.

The referee rises to the demands of the game. He is in on every play. Some games require more effort than others, but the limits do not change. Refereeing does not interfere with his personal fulfillment: It is part of it. He does not bemoan the fact that he is not a spectator: He relishes the job.

Like refereeing, guiding children can be a tough job or an easy job on any given day. It depends on the mood of the children, whom they are with, the importance of the problems that come up, and even the weather. On some days, all goes smoothly, and no one is stepping over the limits or challenging the calls. On other days, you blow the whistle constantly and are called upon to make some debatable decisions.

Parenting is not something that interferes with your personal life—it is part of it. It will be impossible for you to truly enjoy your children if you view them as an interruption of peace and joy. Also, if parenting is "the work" you do instead of a lifestyle you love, you will always be awaiting the moment when you can "get off work." That attitude will show up in how you treat your children. If God is at the center of your daily life and if you partner with Him in revealing the fruit of the Spirit to your children even during the most difficult times, God will give you the grace to meet the demands of each and every day.

In fact, when a decision needs to be made, some of the work will have already been done because your decisions will be based on limits you have already established for your family. Your decisions and attitudes will also be framed by the Word of God. Just like we never take breaks from serving God, we must always be ready to seize the opportunity to heartily serve others. If our happiness is dependent on circumstances, we will constantly be on an emotional roller coaster. And if that is the case, our children will never know what to expect from us. One day we will be happy-go-lucky, and then when things don't go the way we would like them to, we could act as if life with children were filled with drudgery for us. How about a play on former President Kennedy's words: Ask not what the family can do for you; ask rather what you can do for the family. The apostle Paul put it this way: "And whatever you do, do it heartily, as to the Lord and not to men" (Colossians 3:23).

Parenting should be an expression of our joy in the Lord. This joy can be our source of strength, giving us the appropriate response for whatever challenges may arise throughout the course of a day. Because it is coupled with faith, the joy of the Lord is *not* interrupted by a change in activities, circumstances, responsibilities, or the attitudes of other people. Our joy in the Lord will remain constant if we have been cultivating our relationship with Him. Actually, the Scriptures command us to rejoice and praise Him all of the time (see 1 Thessalonians 5:16). In order for it to be true joy and not just pretense, it must be a result of our companionship with the Lord all day long.

It is important for you to schedule time for being alone with God, relaxing, having fun and interacting with other adults, and going on dates with your spouse. It is impossible to give out of an empty vessel, so parents will need to refuel often. However, when making time for yourself, be sure to keep in mind that your children are your primary responsibility and not interruptions. We can learn a bit about this from Gwen's discovery:

It hardly ever failed. All I had to do was to sit down for a TV show in the evening, and my five-year-old would come up asking me to read a storybook.

I resented it—until I realized my TV watching was like the lifeguard getting a suntan. My primary responsibility was to the children.

So I changed my viewpoint. If I sit down to watch a TV program with children around, I do so expecting to be interrupted. Sometimes I ask my child to wait, or offer some alternative activity until the program is over, or shift him over to Dad. Most of the time, something works.

Otherwise, I put off my TV watching until all the children are in bed—with one exception.

Tuesday night at eight o'clock, my favorite TV show airs. On that night my husband takes the major responsibilities of the evening so I can have that one pleasure…undisturbed and unbothered.

Overall, my kids come first. I am their mother and want to be available.

Sam came to the same realization.

The Saturday or Sunday football game would come on, and I'd sit down to watch it. Like clockwork, here my son Jess, age five, would come with his football, wanting to play catch in the backyard.

At first, it bugged me, and I tried to put him off. Then I realized I had bought him the football. Also, it was a chance to do some teaching.

"I'll play with you for fifteen minutes," I tell him now. That's about all his interest and energy span will allow for. It's time for fellowship and helping Jeff to learn how to handle a football.

So I start out my afternoons planning to play football in the backyard. After we're done and Jess is tired or wants to go to another activity, I sit down and watch the rest of the game. Since the ball game lasts three hours, this doesn't always work out. Jeff may be back.

I am not saying that parents should overindulge their children. However, as we can see from the examples above, parents can be creative about how they can enjoy some of their favorite activities and yet still give their children the attention they need.

ENJOYABLE PARENTING

It is easy to see how in both examples above everyone enjoyed each other even more than they had before. Gwen enjoyed relaxing one night a week while her husband took care of the children, and the children and their father enjoyed some dedicated time together. Sam probably enjoyed watching football even more after he spent time throwing the football around with his son. And certainly little Jess felt included in his dad's hobby of watching football. In fact, the day will probably come when the two of them will watch games together and throw the football around during halftimes.

THE PRINCIPLE OF HELP

Parenthood is helping your children to flourish and be successful in every area of their lives—both today and tomorrow. At first glance, the idea of helping a child may not seem very enjoyable. However, if you lovingly view guiding your children as a form of helping them, even the most difficult days will be more enjoyable.

In this chapter we will examine five strategies for helping children:

1. redirecting unacceptable behavior
2. giving direct assistance when needed
3. giving more help than needed
4. preparing the environment in advance
5. pressure

REDIRECTING

Sometimes children need a lot of help. At other times they just need a nudge in the right direction. Redirecting a child is a wonderful, non-confrontational way to help young children shift their attention away from a circumstance they are unable to cope with at the time.

Liza's mom chose to redirect her young daughter one morning. The three other children in the Hawkins family were quietly watching a television program when little Liza woke up in a bad mood and immediately started pestering them.

It was obvious to Mrs. Hawkins that Liza would need a nap that morning, but it was too early for that. She determined that redirection was the best way to maintain the peace, so she whispered in Liza's ear, "I sure could use your help making pancakes this morning."

Mom then scooped her tired little girl up into her arms and carried her into the kitchen. Liza really did not help much, but she did enjoy stirring the batter that didn't need any more stirring and tasting the first pancake that came off the grill. And before the other children came into the kitchen to eat, Mom had already tucked Liza back into bed for an early morning nap.

This is an example of redirecting unacceptable behavior. Liza's coping skills would probably be much better after she woke up from her nap. Attempts to force her to get along with the other children that morning would have been futile, so her mother decided that the best course of action would be to redirect her to an activity that separated her from the other children. That morning, Liza needed extra loving care and attention from her mother. After getting the rest she needed, she undoubtedly woke up with a big appetite and got along well with the other children. If not, her mom would have to monitor whether or not she might be getting sick and provide her with the extra care and help she needed.

Redirecting is also the best way to settle a dispute between two young children. If two preschool or young school-age children are fighting over a bicycle, the best solution might be to redirect their attention and energy elsewhere. However, if the children have been involved in a heated argument, the tension between them may be so high that the adult will need to stay with the children until they have calmed down and become engaged in another activity. For example, one child could ride the bicycle while you play Ping-Pong with the other child for a few minutes. Or the three of you could throw around the football for a few minutes until the kids have cooled down a bit and are able to play together peacefully.

Redirection alone is usually fine for preschoolers and young school-age children. However, older children, adolescents, and teens will need to talk about ways they can resolve conflicts next time without getting into a heated argument. The adult can readily turn the conflict into an opportunity for the young people to learn conflict-resolution skills. This is important because they will not always be able to walk away from difficult situations, and that is certainly not what the parent would want to train them to do.

GIVING HELP

I was in the living room of a family's home one afternoon when we heard a little boy shouting from the family room, "I hate these filthy, old things." We looked in to find a small child throwing blocks. He was frustrated because he could not stack the blocks. His father moved in quickly and grabbed his hand, saying, "You can't throw blocks."

Then Dad quieted the boy down by just holding him. They sat on the floor together. Dad took two blocks and began showing him how to stack the blocks successfully: "Move the two closer together. Now you put one on top. Move it like this." After the dad had shown the boy how to stack four blocks, the boy no longer needed help stacking the others. Since the father had helped his son work through his frustration and showed him how to be successful in the project he was undertaking, we could return to the living room and engage again in our conversation.

The father could have handled the situation in a number of different ways. For example, he could have demanded that his son stop throwing the blocks and sent him to his room, but then that would not have helped the boy with his frustration and it would not have taught him the skills necessary for being successful at stacking blocks. However, this father recognized that his son needed help. Along with that, he responded in a way that showed that taking care of his son was his first priority. He did not allow the fact that he was entertaining a guest to interfere with his responsibility for comforting his son and showing him how to do something he was unable to accomplish by himself.

This reminds me of the time when I watched a little girl pulling her wagon along the sidewalk, only to have it slip off and get stuck. When the child began to scream, her mother came on the scene and saw the problem. Then as the mother helped the child pull the wagon back up onto the sidewalk, she pointed to the edge of the sidewalk and said, "You were too close to the edge. When the tire gets too close to the edge, it will get stuck. Try to keep the tire farther away from the edge like this...."

Notice that the mother did not angrily take the wagon away from the child because her chat with another neighbor had been interrupted. She recognized this as an opportunity to help her child learn a new skill. It was evident that her child was her first priority.

GIVING MORE HELP THAN NEEDED

Sometimes a parent will give the child more help than needed just because it is fun to do something together. Or sometimes extra assistance is called for when a child is faced with jobs that are cumbersome or scheduled at "tired" times of the day.

An example of giving extra help can be seen in how Loreen's dad helped her clean the family room even though she did not really need his assistance.

Loreen's family had a rule about the family room: Loreen had to clean it up every night before she went to bed.

It did not take long for Loreen's dad to notice that she was a bit overwhelmed with the task even though she could complete it by herself. When he noticed her trudging through her duties, he decided to pitch in and become her cleaning partner for a while. Together they picked up the blocks, one holding the box, the other putting them in.

As a team they stacked the books and put the toys in the toy box. They straightened up the rocking horse and put all the pieces of furniture in their proper places.

Suddenly, cleaning the family room was no longer taxing. Now it was a fun part of the day when father and daughter could be silly or talk about "little things" together. As they worked together, they found new ways for making the job easier. Then, in order to give his daughter a sense of accomplishing this on her own, he began to help less and less. Eventually, she would clean up the room while he sorted through papers and kept an eye on how she was doing.

Ultimately, he only needed to occasionally remind her that it was time to get started on the job. Most of the time she breezed through it by herself, and occasionally he would lend a hand whether she needed it or not.

Loreen's father helped her keep the limits, but he avoided the rigid approach used by another father who had the same rule. Every night this other father stormed through the house and exclaimed, "Where is that girl? She knows she is supposed to clean up the family room every night. It's her responsibility. She's going to do it! Right now!"

This father was far from being creative. It is easy to see that this kind of approach was not conducive to fostering a helping atmosphere where the child experienced her father's kindness while she was learning under the shelter of his love. What was the difference between these two fathers? One father had a loving spirit and the other one did not.

PREPARING IN ADVANCE

Preparing in advance is used by parents who understand their child's abilities and limitations and recognize their child's readiness for new experiences. Even though the child is often unaware that this kind of help is being given, the parents create an environment that encourages the child to develop new skills and discover new abilities. To prepare a learning environment that is developmentally stimulating for the child, parents must take cues from their children. Watch your child for inclinations, interests, and special abilities. Pray for God to show you the special talents He has placed in your child that He wants to be developed. A loving heart, a watchful eye, a listening ear, and a life of prayer will guide you in how to provide an environment that is rich in learning and discovery opportunities for your child.

Preparing the environment for optimal learning experiences is sometimes called *indirect guidance.* This type of helping begins when you attach a mobile to your newborn's crib so he can have the opportunity to develop his visual perception. Later on you may attach toys to his crib that he can bat with his foot and, in so doing, begin to learn about cause and effect. Then when he is moving toward the toddler stage, you may notice him attempting to stack plastic containers that are a little too big for him to handle, so you buy a colorful set of blocks and put them on the floor for him.

As the years go by and you have continued to prepare the learning and discovery environment, you may buy a boom box and microphone for your five-year-old. Then when you hear her singing in her room, you research the idea of having her take voice lessons.

Watch for the developing interests of your child. We saw this in the example of the father who bought his son a football even though the boy did not know how to throw it. Exposing the child to different types of activities will help the child discover his interests and talents. Your adolescent girl may initially balk at the idea of learning how to quilt, but then when you take classes together, she may discover she loves it and remain dedicated to the art of quilting for the rest of her life.

Do not be surprised if your child tries numerous kinds of sports or activities before discovering what best fits his interests and natural abilities. One year your son may want to play football, and the next year he may want to try soccer. In this case, creating the environment for learning would involve discussions about what he would like to try this year. While he may discover early in the season that he does not like baseball after all, it is best to have him finish the season so that he will learn the value of fulfilling commitments to team members. As a cautionary note, however, I do want to say that parents should not allow special-interest activities to consume the family to the point where the child's interests become the new focus of the family. When this happens, the activities become a type of idol, leaving no room for relationships between family members and with God to be nurtured. Be sure to keep priorities in order.

Less structured ways of preparing the environment may include providing art materials, buying a prayer journal and a special pen, setting aside a special day when the whole family goes to the library, or dedicating one day a month to a new cultural experience, possibly an art festival one month and an outdoor play the next.

Teenagers often think they do not need much help, but keeping open doors of communication is often the best way to help them. If you notice your child is anxious about what college he wants to attend, take a trip to the library and look through catalogs together. If your daughter seems to be putting on too much makeup, arrange a special day when she can get a free make-over and learn how beautiful she can be if she puts on just a little makeup.

Have fun exploring new interests together and sharing old ones. In so doing, you will build memories that will last a lifetime.

Along with building memories, remember that you are also shaping future ministries. Those voice lessons may result in a music ministry. The journal may spark an interest in writing for Christian publications. Learning team sports may shape a Christian businessman or woman who will impact the community for Christ.

Watch diligently for interests in working on the mission field, giving to others, praying for the needs of others, or other activities your child may want to be involved in because of a developing love for God.

"THERE'S NOTHING TO DO!"

Another type of advanced preparation involves having a list of activities for the child to choose from. Sometime in your life you have heard these words (or will hear them), "Mom...I don't have anything to do!" A parent can be ready with several acceptable alternatives. If the parent is not ready with acceptable alternatives, the child may actually make choices that are not good ones. Telling a child what he cannot do is not the same as giving a child a range of choices that he can do.

It was clear that one father I was talking with one day had a long list of things he didn't allow his daughter to do. "I don't let my daughter go out with any non-Christians."

"Oh?" was my response.

"Right. And I don't let my daughter..."

He continued on and on until I got the impression that he had only given his daughter a list of activities she could not do, but had failed to tell her anything she could do. My impression turned out to be true. He had not given her any suggestions on what she could do. For example, this father had not provided his daughter with any opportunities for her to meet Christian boys he would allow her to date, nor had he suggested other fun activities she could do with her friends.

How about creating a special area in your house that would be fun for teenagers to hang out in? How about volunteering to coordinate a Christian roller skating night? Maybe you could gather up all of the kids after school and take them out for pizza or invite some of the kids back to the house for spaghetti night.

To finish the job of setting boundaries, parents must enrich the environment that is within those boundaries. Telling a child what he cannot do is the easy part of setting limits. The real personal investment comes into play when the parent takes responsibility for enriching the child's life.

The next time your teenager comes to you and grumbles, "Good grief! There's nothing to do around here. This place is dead!" What will be your reaction? Have a list of choices for him and be ready to invest your time and energy into fertilizing the grass within the boundaries you have set for him. For example:

"Well, you can invite the youth group over for dinner on Sunday."

"I picked up this jewelry-making kit that was on sale today. Maybe Judy would want to come over so the two of you can make some Christmas presents."

"I will take you over to the YMCA on my way to the grocery store."

"I heard there is a volleyball match at the gym this weekend. Do you want to go over and watch it?"

"Why don't you call up Judy and Liza and see if they want to play Ping-Pong in the basement."

"Why don't you make some popcorn for a family game night?"

"If you will help your sister with her homework, I will have time to work on that photo album we were planning to put together some time this week."

"It would be nice to have a special dessert tonight, how about making one for us?"

"I read in the paper that the Boys Club has art classes tonight. I clipped the ad out for you to look at."

PRESSURE AS HELP

At times, parents need to use pressure. One parent asked, "What do I do when my child sneaks out of church?" If he sneaks out, then have him sit beside you next time. That is pressure.

He will probably say, "What's the matter? Don't you trust me?"

The answer is, "No. I can't be sure what you will do when you are out of my sight, so now you will have to earn my trust again."

I was in a Sunday school department one day where a boy, ten or eleven years old, was throwing spitballs at some of the other children. I heard the teacher say, "I wouldn't do that if I were you." The boy just ignored the teacher and kept throwing spitballs whenever she turned away.

Another adult, perhaps the director, came in and observed what was going on. He looked at the boy and said, "That's enough."

The boy looked up at the man, and the man looked down at the boy. The little boy looked at his teacher, and his teacher looked at the man, who just shrugged his shoulders and walked to the other side of the room but kept an eye on the boy. The boy needed some pressure from a confident adult. Even the child was smart enough to realize the man meant what he said and would be sure there were consequences for any more disruption.

It usually helps to have the consequences spelled out very clearly from the very beginning. For example, the first infraction in that particular class could have been a warning. The second infraction could have been being moved to the back of the class. The third infraction could have led to the child's being taken to his parents and his parents being asked to sit with him during class the following week. When children are told clearly and in advance what the rules are and what the consequences for breaking them will be, they know what is expected of them and they know what will happen if they do not comply with the rules. From there, they have a decision to make. However, only one child usually needs to test the three-strikes-and-you're-out rule before the whole class realizes they do not want to be marched into the sanctuary in front of the whole church and then have their parents sit with them in class next week. That is pressure that almost always works for adults who follow through with their plan!

Of course, the parent could leap to the defense of the child, so parents would need to be told the rules in advance of leaving their child in the class. The parent whose first priority is the child will be more than happy to support the teachers who follow through with the plan that everyone has been made fully aware of. This is a wonderful opportunity for parents to model behavior that shows respect for authority.

1. Redirecting is often the simplest way to handle unacceptable behavior and conflict between young children.
2. Giving help as needed is the kind of help the child most frequently needs to accomplish a task.
3. Partnering with the child and giving more help than needed is often the most fun.
4. Preparing in advance creates an environment where children can discover, learn, grow, and flourish. It also implies that the parent enriches the environment that is within the boundaries that have been defined by the parents.
5. Pressure may seem like the most dramatic because it involves consequences. However, if the rules and consequences are clearly communicated to the child in advance, the child knows what is expected and what will happen if he does not comply. Pressure should be applied with caution. But pressure can be applied safely when it is well planned, when communication is very clear, and when the well-being of the child guides the parent's response to the child's noncompliant behavior.

Loving guidance brings bountiful rewards to the child and to the parent. The Bible tells us that "We know that all things work together for good to those who love God, to those who are the called according to His purpose" (Romans 8:28).

Help is part of your child's daily bread, but it is also part of yours. Savor the moments of each day, being nourished in the Lord yourself as you provide nourishment for the children. As they learn, so will you. As they discover, so will you. Each day, new vistas will open up for you as you watch a parade through their eyes, hear birds chirping through their ears, or feel the waves crashing at your feet while you encourage your littlest one to safely venture a few more inches away from the shore.

Sure, it takes a lot of work to pack the family van with snack foods, lawn chairs, an ice chest, sunscreen, towels, a blanket, pails and shovels, water rafts, surfboards, sunglasses, sun hats, diaper bags, changes of clothes, kids, and kids' friends. However, your life is unlike anyone else's. You can push a swing high above the trees while one of the people you love most in the world shouts, "Swing higher, Mommy. Push us higher, Daddy!" Those are the unforgettable moments you will cherish forever.

Oh yes, you may have to let the housework go on Saturday mornings because you are cheering your daughter on as she chases a soccer ball down one field. Then you may only have time to run home and throw in a couple loads of laundry before you run back to the school to cheer your son on as he runs with a football (or marches with his trombone) down another field. But this is your life. It is the life you are building together under the canopy of God's love. The precious moments of your life together should be savored, cherished, well tended, and bathed in prayer. Setting the boundaries in which your family safely lives is just the beginning. It is what you do within those boundaries that will warm your heart and theirs for a lifetime.

Even on those days when the kids are sick, tired, cranky, or testy, you can rejoice in the knowledge that as you point your child toward the pathway of righteousness and a close relationship with the Lord, you will be compelled to dip into the wellspring of His grace. Keep in mind that the blessings are not limited to watching sunsets together. The challenges and heartaches of parenthood are an integral part of the blessing. Seeking His guidance and presence during difficult times is often what brings us closer to Him—and to each other.

9

DEALING
WITH
RESISTANCE

THOUGHT STARTER

Children know how to test their parents' hearts: Resist.

MEMORY VERSE

"If you are willing and obedient,
you shall eat the good of the land;
but if you refuse and rebel, you shall be devoured."

ISAIAH 1:19-20

WHY DO OUR CHILDREN RESIST SOME OF OUR LIMITS after we worked so hard to make them reasonable and reachable?

Remember the essence of human nature: "We have turned, every one, to his own way" (Isaiah 53:6).

To elaborate a little on the characteristics of human nature, here is another biblical insight: "For rebellion is as the sin of witchcraft, and stubbornness is as iniquity and idolatry" (1 Samuel 15:23).

"I won't." Who has not responded this way? It is as though we were bewitched. In this mood, it is as though we idolized our own ideas and were ready to take on the whole establishment.

Limits reveal the spirit. They do not cause it. It is normal and natural to want to do things the way you want to do them. Therefore, the parent should not be surprised when a child is persistent in wanting to do what he wants to do.

Adults are the same way. For instance, how long must a business manager supervise the staff? As long as the business is open. As long as the employees are the manager's responsibility. This is no problem for the manager if she accepts the fact that resistance exists, and she accepts the responsibility for dealing with it.

God's Word does not teach us to fulfill the desires of our children. God says to train them in the way that they should go. God does not imply that they will welcome your training. In fact, they may stubbornly disagree with you every step of the way. Remember, you are the trainer; they are the trainees. As such, even though the children may have some input on what the rules will be, you have the final say!

EXPECT RESISTANCE TO TRAINING

Generally speaking, children are not delighted with limits on their behavior. Trying to keep your children smiling all day long would be a futile venture. If you have realistic expectations and know that there will be times when your children will balk when you ask them to do something, you will not be caught off-guard when it happens.

A lady once asked me, "How do you get your children to do what you want them to do without getting angry at them?"

She had a teenage daughter whose job was to empty the dishwasher.

Her mother would call out, "The dishes are ready," in a nice voice. (No child.)

She would call out again, "The dishes are ready." (Nothing happened.) Then, "The dishes are *ready!*" (Still no movement.)

"Did you hear me?" (Now at a shout.) The *dishes* are *ready!*" (Still no child.)

By then, the mother told me, "I'm so mad I wipe my hands and go into the living room screaming, *"You get out there and take care of those dishes!!"* (At last the girl does it.)

"How can I get her to do the dishes without me getting so mad at her first?" the mother asked.

I said, "Lady, do me a favor. Tomorrow night, when the dishes are ready, you call out just as nice as you know how, 'The dishes are ready,' and then march into the living room and make sure it happens immediately."

She did.

What a surprised child her daughter was. Imagine Mother meaning what she says when she is in a good mood! What had happened here was that the little girl had discovered her mother was not serious until she was fighting mad. Until then, the girl did not feel she needed to pay attention. This mother had two problems at work at once: (1) dealing with her child's resistance and (2) dealing with her own response to the child's resistance. The simple solution was for the mother to enforce her first pleasant call rather than let the situation escalate as she progressed to her fourth angry call. Otherwise she would have continued to teach her daughter the art of noncompliance.

"DAD, YOU SHOULD TAKE BETTER CARE OF..."

Obviously your children will not resist all limits. For example, our son was overjoyed when he was assigned the duty of keeping the car clean.

This was a responsibility he liked having because he wanted to keep the car clean, so much so that he was always nagging me, "Dad, you should take better care of the car." I could see it was time for delegation of duties, and he was more than happy to oblige.

From this example we can see that it helps to assign duties to your children that they will enjoy doing. Duties do not always have to be work and work alone. They can also be fulfilling for the child. If Suzie loves baking, assign her to keep the cookie jar stocked. If Joleen organizes things well, assign her the task of managing the kitchen drawer clutter. On the other hand, duties may also be assigned to help a child learn or practice a certain skill. For example, if it is time for Terence to learn how to change the oil in the car, then assign him to help Dad with that job on Saturday.

REASONS DO NOT OVERCOME RESISTANCE

Wouldn't it be great if your children would simply obey after you explained to them why you wanted them to do what you ask?

Children don't usually even hear your reasons when they do not want to do something. The smarter they are, the more ingenious they will be in trying to do what they want to do. At this point they do not want your attention: They want their own way.

What do they need? They need a good-humored mother who appreciates the contest and enjoys it. They need a good-humored father who is backing her up and who steps in to help.

MY MOM

I can remember how when I was a teenager I tried to talk my mother into letting me go out after she said I could not go. I approached her with something like this, "Awe, come on, Mom, won't you please let me go out? Please, Mom?"

I tried to make myself look and sound as pathetic as possible, appealing to her sympathy and her motherly instinct. Surely she would concede to someone who was pleading as much as I was.

What do you do with a child who is playing the martyr, one who tries to put on a sincere act and tries to cajole something out of you that is against the limits?

She said no.

"Please, Mom, please let me go out!"

She said no.

I decided there was no use being decent. It was necessary for me to try something else.

"So you say you love me, huh? How could any mother who loved her child treat me the way you are treating me? Can I go?"

She said no.

"But, Mom, everyone else but me is going. You wouldn't want to make a freak out of me, would you? Can I go?"

Once more, the same answer.

What else could I think of? You see, my objective was to get out of there any way possible—whether through lying, flattery, or whatever.

But my best line was always playing the role of the victim. I figured my trump card was always this line, "So you call yourself a Christian. How could any Christian mother treat me like this? Can I go?"

She did not burst into self-defense. She had respect for my attempts to resist her plan. All she said was no.

That used to make me so angry! I would retaliate by using all the ingenuity and creativity I could come up with to make life miserable for my mother until I went to bed.

Sound familiar? When I was defeated, I would go to bed thinking, "How does a fellow get saddled with a parent like that? Boy, if only I would die, then she'd be sorry." I pictured myself in a coffin, my mother looking down at my dead body. In my imagination, I fired this thought off toward my grieving mother: *Serves you right!*

There was no point in appealing to Dad. He would just back Mom up. Yet in my better moments I was aware that they loved me. I sensed that they had an attitude of approval and a real affection for me.

After I grew up, married, and had some children, I was amazed when I heard some of the same reasoning come out of the mouths of my own children. My children were saying the same things I had said years earlier to my own mother, the same things your children are probably saying to you.... "Look what you are doing to me! A nice man like you, do you want to ruin my life?"

Children sometimes fervently want something they should not have. Yes, parents must respect their children and take their wants into consideration, but the decisions must finally be based on what is in their best interests.

AFFECTION

The Bible says it so simply: "Be kindly affectionate to one another with brotherly love, in honor giving preference to one another" (Romans 12:10).

A FIGHTING LIGHTWEIGHT

I once observed raw human nature in the living room of a lovely home. A four-year-old was pounding a three-year-old over the head. No adult had heard what went on before the beating started, so no one knew what led up to the fight. At a time like this, you never find out who started the fight. It is almost impossible. So this is no time for a lecture or questioning. A swift rescue operation is called for. The mother did just that. Without saying a word, she pried the four-year-old off his victim and carried him into the kitchen.

"I hate you," he screamed at his mother. "Leave me alone."

The mother coolly replied, "I know you feel that way, but until you cool off you cannot play with your sister. I'll just wait here with you until you do."

How this mother responded to her child is a picture of where dealing with resistance begins: in affection. No matter what the behavior, affection that portrays tenderness, kindness, gentleness, and firmness must be the starting place for a parent's response to the child's resistance. Affection must be the springboard to basic gentleness and firmness.

Sometimes neighbors must work together. In one case, a little neighbor girl was a biter. You cannot order a small child to stop biting. She was playing in the backyard with the child next door when there was a blood-curdling scream and both mothers came running out of their houses. Sure enough, the neighbor girl had been bitten.

The children were fighting over the swing. The neighbor girl had tried to take over the swing, and the other child had resisted. Biting is a powerful weapon, and she used it. She knew she had done wrong.

One mother hurried to the bitten child to comfort her. The other mother hurried to the one who had done the biting and took her into the house. She said, "You forgot, didn't you?"

"Yeah, I did," the girl replied.

In this case, the little girl was already sorry, and the mother's approach was much more effective than if she had glared at the child and said something demeaning to her.

The biting child's mother went on to remind her child that mothers are there to help. The storm was over. There is no simple solution to such a problem, but normally children who have been biting other children will need closer supervision. This will ensure the other children's safety. A parent or caregiver can generally recognize when a child is becoming frustrated and likely to bite. In this case, within an hour the children were playing happily in the sandbox while one of the mothers stood just a few feet away from them. Within a year, the little girl was no longer biting other children. She had developed her verbal skills to the point where she could communicate her needs, wants, and feelings.

Understanding why a child may be responding in an unacceptable way will help you determine what measures to take. If you have been paying attention to clues about your child's developmental level or special circumstances, you will be able to respond in a gentle but firm manner.

There is a difference between gentle firmness and hostile firmness. A basic affection for the child, no matter what the behavior, is an important building block to parental success.

RESPECT

Respect implies knowledge about the characteristics and needs of the child. What can your child do and what can he not do? Often a parent will be disgusted with a child because the parent is demanding more than the child can produce. To know enough about your child—to know what he can and cannot do—requires constant attention, study, trial, and error. What works with one child may not work with another. For example, a quiet request may be all that is required for one of your children to start getting ready for bed. Another child may need a lot of time to wind down in his room with the lights dimmed before he can easily start getting ready for bed. The second child may need two bedtimes. He may need one for quiet time and the other for lights out.

HELP IN ACCEPTING LIMITS

All children need help in accepting limits from time to time. At different times in their lives they need more help than others. A four-year-old girl is an example of this. Sally's mother, in despair, said, "I am raising a little delinquent." It was easy to see why the mother was feeling this way. Her child had become the terror of the block. This mother was beside herself and did not know where to turn for help. Another parent in the neighborhood gave her the help she needed when she showed her the secret of setting reasonable limits and helping the child observe them.

One day little Sally had scattered blocks all over the room when she was playing at Mr. Brandon's house. Suddenly, Sally got up and started walking toward the closet to get her coat.

The neighbor said, in his firm way, "We should pick up the blocks before you go."

"I'm not picking up any blocks," Sally announced as she marched toward the closet. This little girl needed someone to help her take care of the blocks. Recognizing Sally's need for someone to help her pick up the blocks, Mr. Brandon gently, but firmly, led her back to the center of the room. Because Sally had determined that she was not going to pick up any blocks, she needed extra help. With her hand in his, he picked up a block and put it away. He picked up the second one and the third one.

She said, "Leave me alone. I'll do it myself." He left her alone, but the minute he released her hand, she darted toward the closet. He went after her and brought her back. She was very rebellious and needed some more external help. She did not need a scolding or a threat or a spanking. Those techniques had been tried unsuccessfully by her mother. The neighbor started over again with the child's hand in his. She did not like it. She protested, but they were getting the job done. He was not doing it for her. He was doing it with her. This is a very important principle. Again she said, "Leave me alone. I'll do it myself." He let her hand go. This time she did not run to the closet, but stood there and watched him pick a few blocks up. He took her hand in his again and helped her pick up several more blocks because she still was not willing to do it by herself. Finally she gave in and said, "Leave me alone." He released her hand and sat nearby while she picked up the rest of the blocks by herself. Here we see two kinds of help: (1) He gave her direct guidance when he held her hand while she picked up the blocks, and (2) he provided indirect guidance and support when he sat close to her while she finished the task by herself.

It is true that he did most of the work. It would have been easier for him to do it all himself, but this would not have taught the child what she needed to learn. He did not alienate that child; in fact, his house was her favorite place to play. In his home there were definite boundaries, whereas she did not have the security of known limits in her own home. If she yelled, kicked, and screamed, the parents quieted her down by no longer requiring her to do what they had asked her to do.

A child should not be given her way just because she throws a tantrum. If parents change the limits because the child screams, they are inviting the child to scream again and again as a means of avoiding compliance. Keeping the child quiet and happy cannot be the goal. Helping the child conform, no matter how much she resists it, must be the goal. The primary issue should not be to stop the screaming. A child will continue her tactic of screaming only as long as it produces the results she desires. If your request is fair and reasonable, then, with all kindness, help your child fulfill it.

"TRAIN" YOUR CHILD

A father tells of an incident that arose with his very beautiful daughter. She was offered a contract to become a model. There was only one obstacle in the way. Her dad would have to falsify her age on the contract because she was too young. She came home very happy and enthusiastic about this opportunity. It would mean one hundred dollars a week for her while she was going to high school. Her mind was made up. However, because of his spiritual wisdom and personal integrity, her father refused to allow her to accept the contract. She argued, "Aren't you interested in my future?" She accused him of not loving her and not caring for her welfare. What was he to do? It was a very emotion-packed problem. There was a simple premise pointing to the very obvious solution though: It is not right to lie about her age. He might expect that his daughter would be somewhat less than delighted with his decision. A father cannot always expect his children to appreciate his position. However, he must do the right thing.

God does not teach us to humor the desires of our children. He does say, "Train up a child in the way he should go" (Proverbs 22:6).

God does not even imply in the Scripture above that the child will appreciate your training. The child may even stubbornly resist you every inch of the way. Because the parent is the trainer, he must have some concept of the goals toward which he is working. The day will probably come when the young woman who aspired to be a model will look back on this experience she had with her dad and say, "I'm glad he made that decision." Knowing that she may not fully understand his reasons now, he should be kind, gentle, and patient. His firm allegiance to what he knows to be right and best will help ensure that the development of her own integrity will cause her to someday understand and appreciate his consistent displays of godly character.

We have all gone through periods when we could not have what we wanted and could not understand why. Yet, when we look back through the telescope of the years, discipline and denial make sense. We need not be so concerned with our children's emotional response to our discipline. The most important thing is our wholesome reaction to their reaction.

EXPRESS TRUE LOVE

The mother of a young child asks, "What do you do with a child who deliberately disobeys?" For example, she tells the child not to eat crackers in the living room, but the child takes the crackers and eats them in the living room anyway. Then if she insists on the child's going back into the kitchen, the child begins to cry. The psychology books say you should be sure your child knows that you love her. How do you demonstrate your love? By giving in? Evidently this mother thought this was the case. This little three-year-old had discovered a modus operandi that worked every time. If she looked hurt and shed a tear, her mother would take her up in her arms and say, "I love you. You can eat crackers in the living room." No wonder this girl is a neighborhood problem. Her mother says so, and everybody agrees with her. What should the mother do? She should give her daughter two choices: Eat the crackers in the kitchen or do not eat them at all, regardless of how much the girl pouts. When your child questions your love, realize that you are the one who must teach your child the meaning of real love. The child will think love means giving her everything her heart desires. The parent must teach the child otherwise.

On the other hand, however, if a young child blurts out the truth to a parent who is motivated by resentment and hatred, the parent will need to repent and seek to have the love of God restored in his or her heart. Partnering with God gives the parent the confidence needed to remain steadfast in decisions and affectionate in approach. All of our actions must issue from a wellspring of affection, tenderness, love, kindness, and long-suffering.

MAINTAIN THE RIGHT SPIRIT

A sign posted at the entrance of a popular restaurant read No Shoes, No Service. A group of teenagers, none of whom were wearing shoes, walked past the sign and entered the restaurant. The hostess finally yielded to their charm. Did she do them a favor? A sign that says No Shoes, No Service means nothing if it is not enforced. A law becomes a farce when it is not enforced. What did these youths learn? They found out that if they turned on enough charm and used plenty of persuasion, they could sometimes break the law.

It was an unfortunate lesson for them to learn. When you get something you are not supposed to have, you do not enjoy it. Your own conscience judges that you have no right to it; nevertheless, it is natural to want to violate standards, to cross limits.

SIN IS THE ROOT OF RESISTANCE

The Bible tells us that "All have sinned and fall short of the glory of God" (Romans 3:23).

What is sin? This is a word that many people dislike. Sin is selfishness. This includes bitterness, stubbornness, rebellion, anger, wrath, malice, hostility, and disobedience to parents. As we look upon our tender little ones, they seem clean and pure and innocent. We wish children were as innocent as they look, but we know that in their hearts is the potential for all kinds of sin. They will sulk, pout, throw tantrums, cry, and argue.

CHILDREN ARE SINNERS

In all of my years of counseling, no one has ever presented me with the problem of a child who never disobeys. Did you ever hear of a child like that? To rebel is normal. It is part of human nature. Every time you give birth to a child, he will be disobedient by nature. You may not like this, and the fact may make you feel uncomfortable. You wish it were not true, but both the Bible and experience, however, tell us that it is true. When you set a limit, your child will tend to want to break it. This is as normal as breathing.

In training children we find different degrees of rebellion. The first child may be easygoing, but sneaky. A second child may be a violent rebel. The third child may be a silent rebel. These are all different types of the manifestation of sin. Anyone who has two children will tell you how different one is from the other. You wonder how your training could produce such variations. Anyone who has three children will tell you how different each of them is from the other two! There is not necessarily anything wrong with you or your training. It is just that people are different, and we rebel in different ways and degrees. Some of us can do wrong in the most gracious way.

An example of gracious rebellion was observed in a nursery school. A little boy there had been told not to climb up on a table, but he did so anyway. One of the women was about to scold him and take him off of the table. But he saw her coming, stretched out his arms, and with a big smile wrapped his little arms around her. Then before she could say anything, he said, "I'm sorry." She was about to say, "Get off the table!" Instead, she very gently put him down on the floor. Just as soon as she turned her back, he climbed on the table again. It is important to note here that this child was just as rebellious as the child who might defiantly climb on the table and stubbornly sit there until he is removed.

Over and over, wherever there are children in this world, parents ask, "What am I going to do with my child? He won't listen!" Of course he will not listen, because a little child will try to do what he wants to do. Some children will be pleasant about it, and some will be objectionable about it. Either response manifests the same principle—man tends to rebel.

If you put two or more children together to play and leave them alone without any adult supervision, it will not be long before there is a conflict. Conflict among people in every age group is just as normal as breathing.

THE CURE FOR RESISTANCE

While you are rearing your children, keep in mind that they need the Savior. They must find the power of God that will enable them to live right. You can control your children with stares, threats, promises, rewards, and many other techniques. The only effective control, however, is for the child to be motivated by a love for God—not only by a love for you or a fear of you.

A mother, speaking of a son who had gotten into some trouble, said, "I am so glad he didn't tell me about these terrible things he did until I returned from my trip. It would have spoiled my vacation." By making this statement in front of him, she essentially told him that her happiness depended upon whether or not he behaved himself.

You must have a much better reason than this for asking your children to conform. If you use the threat of your own unhappiness, you deny the very essence of being and living as a Christian whose trust is in the Lord.

As you teach your children the ways of God, they will learn them best by seeing them demonstrated in you (see Philippians 4:5–7). Peace, comfort, consolation, and joy are not just beautiful words. They should be your daily experience by faith in God through the Lord Jesus Christ. If this is so, these qualities should be demonstrated in you even when your children are resisting your training.

LIMITS AMOUNT TO RESPONSIBILITIES

When limits are obeyed adequately, they form a basis for granting privileges. Privileges should be deserved before being granted and should be withdrawn if the accompanying responsibilities are not fulfilled. For example, two girlfriends, both fourteen, like to alternate weekends at each other's houses. This privilege is based on whether or not homework and duties around the house are completed.

If a privilege is no longer deserved or if a request cannot be granted, the decisions should be made promptly and forthrightly. A child of any age can accept a negative answer much easier than he or she can wait for a postponed answer. Unless new facts are introduced, a decision should not be reversed if both the child's and the adult's points of view have already been taken into consideration.

There is a big difference between rights and privileges. Teenagers are inclined to regard certain privileges as their rights. The parent can clearly communicate what activities are privileges that may be earned or revoked, regardless of whether or not the teenager thinks the activity is his or her "right." Again, the child must know what to expect in advance. For example, a teenager may think the use of the family car is a right, but a parent can clearly state that it is a privilege that must be earned and may be revoked. Curfew time may also be regarded as a privilege that may be adjusted to any earlier or later time. Clothing and entertainment allowances should also be earned.

Threats of punishment that cannot be enforced must be carefully avoided. Certainty of punishment is more important than the nature of the punishment. Empty threats encourage disrespect for the parents and for all authority.

One sixteen-year-old boy asked to take the car to the store a few blocks away. His father agreed on condition that the boy come right back. The boy came back an hour later, explaining that he had met some of the guys and got into a rap session. In this case a temporary limit had already been imposed on his use of the car and now he had failed to prove that he would strictly adhere to his father's limit. As a result, he lost his driving privilege for a week.

Similarly, a child who becomes reckless with the car should have parental supervision. The teenager may not like this requirement, but he should not have the privilege of driving the car alone until he proves himself to be more responsible behind the wheel. This is a limit that must be imposed for his safety and for the safety of others. No amount of a child's balking should ever lead to a parent's withdrawing the true love that is exhibited when he takes measures that will further ensure safety. In this case, the very life of the child, not to mention the lives of others, is at stake.

ATTENDING CHURCH

What if my child does not want to attend church? The first issue is your own conviction—are you convinced of the value of church? Do you believe that bringing your children under the influence of a local church is a positive and constructive thing to do? If you do believe this, you should do whatever is necessary—whether he is eight or eighteen—to get him to church.

Of course, it would also be wise to find out why the child resists attending. Maybe by watching your life, he thinks church attendance is worthless. Perhaps you could give him some practical tips on how to get more out of a church service. Be realistic by admitting that you do not always seem to profit by every service, but that you firmly believe that a person can find strength and reassurance and develop a closer relationship with God through being actively involved in a local church.

Some of the Scriptures to refer to during these discussions may include those listed below. If your child's reading and comprehension level is high enough, ask him to read these verses and explain to you what he thinks they mean. Then help him determine how the Scriptures apply to his own life.

- "All have sinned and fall short of the glory of God" (Romans 3:23).

- "Not forsaking the assembling of ourselves together, as is the manner of some, but exhorting one another, and so much the more as you see the Day approaching" (Hebrews 10:25).
- "Children, obey your parents in the Lord, for this is right" (Ephesians 6:1).
- "Children, obey your parents in all things, for this is well pleasing to the Lord" (Colossians 3:20).

If physical help is needed, your spirit should be one of love and firmness. Your motive is not, you will do this *because I said so;* but, you will do this *because it is a good thing to do.* Your children should clearly realize that you have a responsibility from God to train them in the way that they should go. Whether your children are teenagers or preschoolers, they will need your help in accepting limits.

For younger children, you may have to demonstrate and make positive suggestions until they learn to use various limits and principles. One day three children decided to play a game. Each child wanted to be first. An argument led to pushing and pulling until Mother stepped in to help. She knelt down on their level and picked up the spinner. "Here," she said calmly, "let's have the spinner choose who will be first. Susan you spin it first; Freddie is next; and then Tommy. Whoever gets the highest number will be first; the second highest will be second; the third highest will be last. Now isn't that an easy way to decide?" The children agreed and a simple suggestion from a calm and kind adult helped them get past a rough spot and enjoy the game.

Accepting limits will be easier if the parent enforces them firmly and with love. If you say, "Lunch is ready. Get washed and come to the table," be sure lunch is really ready so you will be free to help your children leave what they are doing, wash, and come directly to the table. It is up to you to enforce the limits you set up and to teach your children to carry them out. Failure to carry through on predetermined limits encourages disobedience and promotes the idea that you do not really mean what you say.

A fact that comes up frequently when dealing with parents in the counseling room is that the limits in their home are not mutually agreeable to both the father and the mother.

Naturally, when parents disagree in methods or outlook, the child is caught in the middle. Pleasing both parents at the same time is impossible. Much of the strain on adolescents results from uncertainty about which way to turn because the parents disagree. The apostle Paul wrote: "Fulfill my joy by being like-minded" (Philippians 2:2).

If we will turn to God, He will give us His Spirit of like-mindedness in the matter of limits, standards, and prohibitions.

Parents should keep in mind that their children will face limits all of their lives. At school, in church, and in the community there are limits or laws: dos and don'ts. Children who learn to accept reasonable limits at home can accept the limits placed upon them outside the home.

Uncertainty on the part of an adult about the direction that guidance should take indicates a lack of proper study and consideration. A sure sense of direction that the adult conveys to the child in word and deed is essential for effective guidance. Look at the biblical view as expressed in these three verses:

- "The rod and rebuke give wisdom, but a child left to himself brings shame to his mother" (Proverbs 29:15).
- "Correct your son, and he will give you rest; yes, he will give delight to your soul" (Proverbs 29:17).
- "'As many as I love, I rebuke and chasten. Therefore be zealous and repent'" (Revelation 3:19).

Adults do not do their children any favors when they allow their children to get their own way. By the same token, adults are not giving adequate guidance when the children's opportunities for development are only confined to their interests of the moment. This kind of adult action or inaction is irresponsibility, not guidance.

The results of such an approach may be seen in the case of Beverly. This example shows the high cost of what happens to a girl when her parent lets her get her own way. Even though Beverly had always gotten good grades in elementary school, she sobbed at my desk and said, "I can't do it! I hate school. I hate teachers!"

I learned Beverly was the youngest of four children, the baby of the family. Because of this she had managed to get her way in most things, and the habit had carried over into school.

In the sixth grade she had been chosen to be Scout treasurer after her mother put on a "super feed" for the troop. She was given the lead in the eighth-grade play because her mother engineered it. Everything always came easily for Beverly because her mother could not stand to see her baby hurt.

But this year was different. Dad had been disabled by a heart attack, and Mom went to work. Now she had no time for a "buttering-up party" or to run interference for Beverly. Her mother could not locate the books needed for Beverly's term paper or coax a postponement of the deadline. Because Mom now worked all day long and had laundry, housecleaning, and shopping to do in the evenings, she could no longer help Beverly with her homework.

In the past, Beverly would put on her helpless-looking face, and Mom would immediately spring to her assistance. And when putting on a show of looking helpless did not work, sulking and refusing to try always did. Now it was different. Looking helpless had gotten her an F in social studies, and sulking after school left her standing while the bus pulled off without her.

Mom had failed to guide Beverly in the way she ought to go. She had let her daughter have her own way. This was not child discipline or guidance, it was irresponsibility. Now Beverly was unequipped when her mother could no longer come to her rescue at every turn. She was unequipped with the determination, fortitude, and boldness that was necessary to make things happen herself. Of course, Beverly could not blame her mother for her childishness. I reminded her that Jesus said: "'In the world you will have tribulation'" (John 16:33).

I explained to her that the world would buffet her with schedules, demands, hard knocks, and even persecution for her faith in Christ. But she did not have to fight the battle alone. "But take heart," Jesus had gone on to say, "I have overcome the world."

Beverly would have to grow up in a world that demanded maturity. To her this was a revelation because she had not realized that she had been acting childishly. No longer wanting to be a "baby," she chose to become a happy teenager. Even though Beverly's mother had not allowed her daughter to develop normally, Beverly was strengthened by the Word of God and began to meet life's challenges with gusto.

A child needs parents who possess a conviction strong enough to carry the child along, against resistance or inertia. The decision on how to best satisfy the fundamental needs of a child rests not on the inexperience and inclination of a child, but on the parents' knowledge of the child's needs.

A child does not know what is good for her when she cries for a candy bar, refuses milk, resists sleep, or darts across the street. The adults in her life are responsible for researching, praying about, and observing what is best.

Mr. Main had the problem of dealing with a teenage son who would not go to bed when told. Because of the boy's late hours, his schoolwork suffered, and eventually he contracted an illness. An important cause, the doctor reported, was fatigue. This boy's parents had failed him.

Over time a child must be given more responsibility. For example, a parent will tie a preschooler's shoes until the child's small motor skills are developed adequately enough for the parent to teach the child how to do it himself. This responsibility is then delegated from the parent to the child. As children grow older, more and more responsibility for doing tasks and making decisions is allocated to the child. Children whose parents have given them choices will more easily cope when they face more choices in life. Those who were always told what to do will not have a good foundation for making decisions on their own. On the other hand, children who have been making decisions based on a range of choices will much more easily make good decisions without adult help.

POINTS TO PONDER

Here are some specific ways you may approach your child in a positive manner when he or she needs your help:

Physical and Verbal Approach

When there is a disturbing incident among children, go to the scene in person. Such incidents are seldom a life-and-death matter, so arrive at the scene in a relaxed and casual manner. It is possible to move rapidly without appearing hurried or upset. There is usually no need to get there at top speed, all out of breath and with your hair flying.

Give thought to your first words. Even if the children are screaming and hitting, you can take a few seconds to consider what you will say or do when you get there. Tone of voice and choice of words are important. You can speak firmly, but in a kind way.

Make eye-to-eye contact. It helps to be on the same level with the person to whom you are speaking. You need not stand over your children, looking down on them so that they have to look up at you. If they are young, scoop them up in your arms or kneel down next to them. If your teenager is sitting down on the couch, sit down next to her.

Attitudinal Approach

What led up to the situation? Often, parents bear down on children, having no plan or approach. If you are to be most helpful, you need to try to find out what happened. As you drew near to the group in question, you may have seen the whole situation or you may not have. Your first priority will be to ensure that the fighting stops so that everyone involved is safe; then it is important to determine if anyone has been physically hurt. Settling the dispute must be secondary to ensuring the safety of the children. The next step will be to separate the children and calm them down. Talking to them individually will probably be the best way to assess the situation. The goal in the resolution of the difficulty will be to help the children find alternate ways of dealing with conflict next time. These kinds of scenarios can be opportunities for teaching and for helping the children.

Remedy the situation. Action must be taken with or without knowledge of all of the facts. If you lack information, be aware of your lack of knowledge. Perhaps the children were too loosely supervised in the first place. Were no adults around to see what was happening until after the outburst had occurred? If so, do not jump to conclusions. After assessing the situation, ask the children how they could have responded to the situation differently. Talk through a number of different alternatives with them. Remember that your firm, kind manner will be the key to turning the situation into a learning experience. Examine each child's needs at that particular moment. Maybe one of them will need to stay close to an adult so he can feel safe or be in control of his feelings. Another child may need to be redirected to a quiet activity. Consequences may include making the disputed equipment off-limits for a specific amount of time or having the children sit alone for a while so they can think about the situation.

Trial and error. Your first attempt may or may not be successful. What works with one child will not work with another. Also, you may not always make perfect decisions, but you can be guided well by your intention to do what is best for the children. The final result may not always mean happiness for all concerned, but the parent can help a child work through frustration. For example, your child might tearfully sob, "I want that truck." But he cannot have the truck just now, so you may need to redirect him to something he can do until then. Or the teenager may be upset because her telephone privileges are removed for a week, but this might be a good time to help her develop a habit of making daily entries in a prayer journal.

Acceptance of children's negative reactions in tense moments. When the incident is over, do not condemn the child by continuing to bring up the subject. Do leave the doors of communication open, though, because the child may want to talk about what happened and ask your advice about what to do the next time a similar situation arises. Your child will be looking for signs that you have forgiven him. Make sure he knows you have not withdrawn your love.

10

SUPERVISION

THOUGHT STARTER

*Supervision involves setting limits,
dealing with resistance, and giving help.*

MEMORY VERSE

*My son, keep your father's command. . . .
When you roam, they will lead you;
when you sleep, they will keep you;
and when you awake, they will speak with you.*

PROVERBS 6:20, 22

SETTING LIMITS...DEALING WITH RESISTANCE...GIVING
help. If we were to put them together and give them one name, that
name would be *supervision.*

A CHAMPIONSHIP COACH

Supervision should be considered a positive activity. To help explain this
point, I will tell you about my basketball coach. We had a championship
team one year because we had a championship coach. All of us on the team
regarded him with admiration and affection. Occasionally, we dreaded him.

For me, dread came when he watched me practice. A player wants to look good when the coach is watching, and I was no different. Whenever he was watching me during practice, I tried to get the ball and take a hook shot: This was the best part of my game.

Did that satisfy him? No, he always came up with the same dreaded sentence, "Good shot. Now let me watch you dribble."

Dribbling was the worst part of my game. If you were to have described me as a basketball player, you would have said my footwork was good, my teamwork was good, my passing was good, and my shooting was good. But what did the coach concentrate on? My dribbling!

Yes, he knew my abilities, and he must have thought I was a good basketball player because I was an integral part of a championship team. But as a wise coach, he quietly watched and firmly insisted on correcting the weak side of my game while he continued to develop my strong side. Of course, before the year was up, I became a good dribbler. This is an example of how working to strengthen an area of weakness, while continuing to develop an area that is already strong, can yield optimum results.

WHAT THE BOSS INSPECTS

There is a saying in the business world: "The employee will do what the boss inspects—not what he expects."

In the restaurant business, the supervisor's job is to meet pre-arranged labor and food costs, standards of cleanliness, customer satisfaction, and more. For the business to succeed, the restaurant manager constantly inspects and balances all of these components in a way that ensures a healthy bottom line.

A coach is also an inspector. My coach's attentiveness to detail brought us to the healthy bottom-line of having a championship team. Evidently my coach had learned that a basketball player will do what the coach inspects, not what he expects.

Parents will also learn quickly that a child will do what a parent inspects, not what he expects. Until the child has developed a strong relationship with the Lord and chosen to be accountable to Him, a parent must be continuously and directly involved in helping the child make good choices. Even the older child, who is striving to please the Lord in all things, will need parental supervision. The older child may have wonderful intentions, but still lack experience and wisdom—that may only be acquired as one grows older.

Younger children will need you to physically help them with dressing, eating, playing, carrying out simple tasks, or obeying limits that will keep them safe. Older children need you to supervise their activities, provide them with reasonable choices that fall within the range of established limits, and encourage them to look for ways to strengthen their relationship with the Lord.

FROM SANDBOX TO CURFEW: HAVE REASONABLE EXPECTATIONS

Supervision ensures that the child stays within the established boundaries. Sometimes parents find out that their children need more supervision than they have given them. I introduced this idea when I referred to the fact that sometimes conflict springs up between children because they lack the adult supervision they need. Lack of supervision was also indicated one day when a young mother put her toddler in a sandbox, gave her a little shovel, and went into the house. Before leaving the child alone outside, the mother said, "Now, you stay there till I come back."

When the mother came back a little while later, she found the child happily digging in the flower bed. This mother discovered that she must either watch to make sure the child stayed in the sandbox or find another way to protect her flowers. Respect for flowers was too much to ask of a toddler. Along with that, a child of this age should certainly not be left outside alone.

Another mother found she needed to provide her three-year-old with more supervision when she tacked a sheet of paper on the wall and sweetly said to her child, "This part of the wall is for you to color on." The mother had read somewhere that this was a good activity for young children and this was the way to do it. She returned in a half hour, and to her dismay, she found Ricky had torn down the paper and was very seriously and busily covering the wall with a preschooler's design. She learned a lesson at the expense of a new wallpapering job. What was the lesson? Small children need close supervision and certainly should not be left alone.

Reasoning with the child who has limited verbal communication and cognitive skills is not an effective substitute for supervision. Another mother learned this. As she tenderly put a coat on her six-year-old Ruthie, the young mother carefully explained to her that the spring air was very crisp and this coat would help keep Ruthie warm. Because the mother thought Ruthie understood this explanation, she happily returned to her housework. A little while later when she caught a glimpse of Ruthie playing outside, she saw that the little girl was only wearing a flimsy blouse. The coat was on the grass, soaking up the spring dampness. Ruthie had not understood her mother's concern over her health. By Ruthie's assessment, now that she was feeling quite warm, the coat was no longer needed. The result? Ruthie caught a cold that lasted for days. Ruthie misunderstood what her mother had said. Her mother's attempt at explaining the necessity of wearing the coat had an effect that was opposite from what she had intended. Along with this, the mother needed to supervise Ruthie more carefully in order to be sure she continued to wear her coat while she was outside.

Whose responsibility was it? The child had either disobeyed or completely misunderstood what her mother had told her. In either case, she had assumed that getting too warm warranted taking off her coat. Her mother learned she could not rely on reasoning alone and needed to more closely supervise her daughter.

SUPERVISION SOMETIMES REQUIRES DEMONSTRATION

Suppose you are watching your children and some of their friends as they play on the playground, and one child says, "Hey, I'm going to try out the slide."

Another says, "Hey, me too!"

Then, just like that, everyone discovers the slide and converges on it all at once. They knock each other down and push some of the smaller children to the back of the crowd. To bring some order to the situation, you go over and select two or three of the children to go down the slide first.

"Now, Wanda will go first, then Mike, and then Joe." As you say this, you also show them how to line up and take turns in an orderly fashion.

It may take time and careful supervision before the children line up and take turns without adult help, but the adult who is watching carefully can anticipate the situation before the confusion happens, remind the children that they will need to line up, and show them how to take turns. Until they have learned to consistently do this without adult help, the children may continue to converge on pieces of equipment from time to time—all at once: Kids will tumble everywhere and trample on each other.

The adult will probably need to repeatedly demonstrate this to young children because cooperation is a social skill that must be learned, and therefore must be taught.

TOO MUCH TIME?

I can almost hear you saying, "You have got to be kidding! Do all that? Spend that much time?"

Well…yes. That is, if you want to put together that perfect play.

Look for a moment at the area of eating. When you first begin to teach your child how to feed herself, she will not have developed her fine motor skills enough to coordinate her index finger and her thumb. Until she begins to show signs that she may be ready to hold a spoon and guide it to her mouth, you will handle the spoon for her and feed her. A lot of supervision and help is needed when you first begin to guide her hand (and the spoon) to the food and up to her mouth. The time will come when you allow her to try it on her own, but before giving her the spoon you will probably put an extra-strength bib on her and cover the floor underneath her with newspaper.

Little by little, she will progress. Once she has mastered the use of a spoon, it will be quite some time before she will be ready to use a fork and a dull knife. There are many skills for a child to learn, but it is important to keep the many step-by-step educational processes in perspective. Each spill, each messed tablecloth, and each soiled outfit is a part of that particular learning process. Of course, not every skill that is learned involves a spoon, but there will be different kinds of messes all along the way. It is all part of the learning process of growing from babyhood into adulthood—and although the overall learning process is a very long one, there is much joy as you proceed with your children over the many hills you happily conquer together.

REDUCING THE ODDS

Adequate supervision involves staying with the task at hand over a long period of time. As the child grows older, the types of supervision the child needs will change, but supervision will still be required. Remember, the Bible says that "We have turned, every one, to his own way" (Isaiah 53:6).

I believe one of the most important helps we gave our teenagers was making sure that their mother or I was always there to greet them when they came home after being out at night—even though they did not like being greeted.

When your children realize you will be there to greet them when they come home, it is quite an encouragement for them to observe limits. Our children would often say, "Why are you always waiting for me?"

The answer was simple, "We love you. We are interested in you. We want to know what you have been doing, that's all. We want to make sure you got home when you said you would."

The older your children become, the more they need your personal supervision and the more they will resist it. I have seen teenagers get into trouble because their parents allowed them to have a party at their house without adult supervision. The parents took off, leaving the large group of teenagers unsupervised. It is important to note that parental supervision removes temptations.

Adequate supervision does not leave room for children and teenagers to continue to disobey. But the parents must also enforce the limits. If not, the parents will be teaching the children to be noncompliant. This can be seen in the example of a child asking her mother for permission to go somewhere.

"Sure," Mom replies, "you can go as long as you promise to be home at ten o'clock."

The daughter agrees but does not show up on time.

"I wish you would listen to me," says the mother. "I want you to come home at ten o'clock."

"Yes, Mom. I just forgot."

"Okay. Now, next time I want you to be home by 10 o'clock."

The next time the teenager goes out, she decides she has a fifty-fifty chance of getting away with going home late. She deducts that a fifty-fifty chance is worth gambling on, so the child pushes a little harder and comes home a little later this time. Much to the teenager's relief, the parents are not even there when she comes home late. As the child slips into the house, she lets out a sigh, "Whew, I got away with that one."

The next time she goes out, she figures she has a sixty-forty chance of getting away with staying out late. When she comes in at 10:45 P.M., her mother gives her another lecture about coming home on time. Ultimately, the girl realizes that if she can just put up with the lecture every time, she can set her own curfew. This kind of supervision is far from adequate and clearly ineffective. In fact, it is better not to set limits you do not plan to enforce. Why? Because you are teaching your child to lie and cheat her way around the limits.

LACK OF SUPERVISION COULD CHANGE YOUR CHILD'S LIFE FOREVER

Parents come to me and plead, "Please, Dr. Brandt, could you help us break up this romance between our daughter and her boyfriend? They have very little in common and are both immature, but they insist on getting married."

I ask, "How long have they been dating?"

"About ten months."

"If this match has been acceptable for ten months, what is wrong with it now?" I prod.

"It hasn't been acceptable, but we didn't want to upset our daughter or appear narrow-minded. We had hoped something would happen to break it up."

These parents did not adequately supervise their daughter. Early on, they had made a decision that was the opposite of their best judgment. Obviously, your children will marry someone they know. So you need to be careful who they know.

Lack of needed supervision is a form of hindering, not helping, the child. A parent's commitment to supervising their children and teens will help ensure their safety and well being.

11

THE TRUTH
ABOUT
CONSEQUENCES

THOUGHT STARTER

*We do our children a great favor if we help them understand
there are consequences for their actions…good and bad.*

MEMORY VERSE

*Do not be deceived, God is not mocked;
for whatever a man sows, that he will also reap.*

GALATIANS 6:7

DISTRAUGHT PARENTS OFTEN COME TO ME BECAUSE THEIR
children are suffering the consequences of not being adequately supervised. Of course, teenagers do not want to be supervised, but oftentimes
dire consequences will be the result of parents adhering to their children's complaints and demands for more personal freedom in areas
where they are unable to cope with temptation.

This was particularly evident when a set of parents came in with
their pregnant daughter.

"I told her she was seeing too much of that boy," wails the mother,
"but she wouldn't listen. She would say, 'Mother, don't you trust me?' I

wanted my daughter to know I trusted her, and look what happened."

What happened? The normal consequences of allowing a young couple too much unsupervised freedom is what happened.

"What can I do?" pleaded another mother. "For an hour or two a night my daughter and her boyfriend sit in his parked car out in front of our house. She tells me there is no reason for me to be concerned, and she refuses to come in."

"Why are you so suspicious, Mother?" she says. "You don't need to worry about us."

If you ask me, the parents should do something. There is a basis for concern. Her daughter surely is not reviewing Bible verses night after night for an hour or two out there. We all know what goes on in a parked car in the dark. How do you get the daughter out of the car?

One possibility rapidly comes to mind. If all else fails, you go outside, open the car door, reach in, and help her out of the car.

"Won't that embarrass her?" Yes, it will. But this is a consequence of defying you.

"Won't she be angry?" She will be furious. But that's her problem, not yours.

"What if she does not come home and parks somewhere else?" Then do not allow her to go. You may also need to deal with the boy and/or his parents.

Give her the supervision she thinks she does not need! Remember, this is your beloved daughter. But the ecstasy of physical closeness at her age is too tempting for her to handle. She needs your supervision and your help. The boy also needs your supervision and his parents' help. Ignoring your parental responsibility at this time can be a poorly matched marriage, or in the very least you will be allowing behavior that your child knows is risky and degrading. Along with this, parents of teenage boys should also be making every effort to ensure that the boys are supervised.

In their teenage years, your children need your guidance and help most. They may not appreciate it now, but they definitely will when they realize five years from now that their lives were not sidetracked by a mistake they would not have been able to undue. Always keep in mind that children lack wisdom and self-control, so when parents leave them unsupervised, the children will be prone to make foolish choices.

A BAD BREAK...OR?

Life will always bring some tough breaks and some good ones. Either way, we must make the most out of the consequences.

One young athlete failed to do this when he grabbed all the football headlines in high school and went off on a scholarship to a university. There he did very well his first year. The consequences of that were praise, newspaper headlines, girls wanting to date him, and parties.

How did he react to his consequences? He reacted by not doing his schoolwork. The result—he became ineligible to play football.

He enjoyed the acclaim all right, but he did not like the consequences of his choice not to study. He even blamed other people for his choice. Although he blamed his teachers for being too hard on him, the real reason why he was unable to play was directly related to the fact that he did not study. Then, because he did not take responsibility for his own choices, he disappeared from sight and dropped out of school, griping all the way about what a tough break he had received. He became a bitter kid, running away from reality. He was not ready to accept the consequences of life and of his own choices...the good with the bad.

Another athlete responded very differently when he was confronted with similar choices. When he went to college to gain an education and play baseball, his outstanding ability and hard work made him a star on the baseball diamond. But because studying was his first priority, he also excelled academically and was encouraged to enroll in a dental school.

As he continued to excel in his dental school studies, he was also signed by a major league ball team that consistently won their way to the championship playoff games. However, becoming a star on this major league team did not detract him from continuing with his studies during the off-season. Because of his dedication to both areas, he had a career ahead of him in dentistry—after he retired from professional baseball.

Both of these athletes were faced with the same choices, but each of them chose very different paths. Both of them received the consequences of their individual choices, and both of them were rewarded accordingly.

CONSEQUENCES...GOOD AND BAD

As we have repeatedly stated throughout this book, our job as parents is to point our children in the right direction. To do that, we need to plan consequences that will help them along the way. Some people call them rewards...or punishment. The consequences we give them today will prepare them to make the right choices that will lead to the right consequences tomorrow. When I think of rewards or punishments, I look at them as consequences—good or bad. People make the choices and suffer—or enjoy—the consequences.

Adults know that the consequences of getting good grades equate to a better chance of getting a suitable job or enrolling in college. In essence, adults understand that good grades usually result in more knowledge about life.

We also know that the consequences of learning to be cooperative are leadership positions, promotions, and raises. On the other hand, the consequences of poor grades and poor cooperation are trouble, missed opportunities, difficulty in getting a job, and difficulty in getting into college. However, long range objectives like college, jobs, promotions, and raises do not interest children. This is because they do not have the experience necessary to see the correlation between what they do now and what opportunities will be (or not be) open to them decades later.

Adults, on the other hand, know these cause and effect relationships are real. Our own experiences and our observations of the experiences of other people have taught us that all choices and experiences yield consequences. We also know that someone else's choices can affect us. For example, we all know of people who have suffered terrible bodily injury and financial reverses because a drunk driver ran into their car. The consequences, in other cases, may be less severe and yet very real. A friend of mine, for instance, lost his business because he guaranteed someone else's banknotes. The notes were defaulted, so the bank held my friend responsible and he ultimately lost his business.

Lecturing our children about consequences they cannot understand is futile, but we can teach them about cause and effect on their own levels by associating short-term consequences with acceptable or unacceptable behaviors. For example, the child may be told: if you do not study, you cannot go out to play. Or…if you practice hard enough, you will have a much better chance at making the team. The first consequences the child experiences will often be those you have established, but in most cases he will also experience natural consequences from his social group.

For instance, you may allow your child to go outside after he finishes his homework, but he will also experience the benefit of receiving good grades from his teachers. Or you may allow your child to watch television after she practices her piano lesson, but she will also experience the benefits of her efforts in the applause and feelings of accomplishment she experiences at her piano recital.

When at all possible, have the consequences be directly related to your child's actions. If you allow your teen to use the car, and he brings it back in good shape, you can be lavish with your praise. If he brings the car back dirty, he may have to wash and vacuum out the car and give up his next turn to drive it. This will teach him that his choices have consequences that are directly related to his behavior.

If your daughter goes where she said she would go and comes home at the designated time, then you are lavish with your praise. If she does not go where she promised or does not come back when she said she would, she may need to pass up the next event at school.

If your son takes good care of his bike, he is entitled to your praise. If he does not, he is grounded from riding it for a day. Again, the parent capitalizes on the opportunity for the child to learn about cause and effect relationships.

TEACH CONSEQUENCES
BY OBSERVING OTHERS

There are other ways for teaching about consequences or cause and effect. For instance, you do not need to let your child ruin his bike before he learns a valuable lesson about the consequences of not taking care of his bike. Instead, you can point out to your child how the neighbor boy ruined his bike because he did not take care of it. You may say something like, "You know, Sam always wants to borrow your bike because he has already ruined his."

Certainly, you also do not let a little toddler wander out into the street and get hit by a car so that he can learn the consequences. You can point out a dead animal beside the road and tell the child why it was killed.

A teenager may not understand why you do not let him run around with undesirable friends. But before long, some of those kids will have been in enough trouble for you to be able to easily point out the dangers of following their lead. And clearly, it makes no sense to let a child learn the hard way about something that could lead to a pregnancy, a sexually transmitted disease, arrests, or drug and alcohol abuse. You can point out what happened in other children's lives.

Life around us is full of lessons to be learned. Unfortunately, some of them are very sad and very tragic. One such example happened when there was a terrible crash down the street from our house. When we ran down to the corner to see what had happened and who was involved, we saw two cars that were completely mangled and four young people who were bloody and broken. The teenagers had been playing chicken with the cars, seeing who would veer away first to avoid a head-on collision with the other car; but when they had come to the corner, neither driver would alter his course.

My wife and I used this tragedy as a teaching situation. Here were young people who had access to a car and all the freedom they wanted, but six months after the accident one of them was still in the hospital and certainly had no freedom at all.

Another tragedy occurred soon after this one. One of the boys in our community had always gotten his own way by being cantankerous and uncooperative, and when he became a teenager he applied his usual sullen techniques to convince his father to buy him a fast car. His father used money as a means of trying to encourage the boy to be cooperative and unselfish. But the very first week the boy had the car, he wrapped it around a pole at high speed and killed his buddy—the consequence of giving a hostile boy a fast car! We used that as a warning.

I believe the response of the parents should be, "If you're angry and hostile at the world, you can't use the car. Around here, only pleasant and gracious people—who exhibit thankfulness—use the car."

In our home, losing the privilege of driving the car became one of the consequences for exhibiting uncontrolled anger. We knew that if we did not teach our children about consequences, they would have to learn about them when they were older. We knew we were helping them to avoid a lot of present and future pain if—early in their lives—we allowed them (or helped them) to suffer or enjoy the consequences of their choices. We pointed out examples of other children's good or bad consequences, but we also supplied our own consequences within our home life. We also did not intervene when they were suffering natural consequences within their own social group.

Here are some pertinent Bible verses:

And you, fathers, do not provoke your children to wrath, but bring them up in the training and admonition of the Lord.

EPHESIANS 6:4

My son, do not despise the chastening of the LORD, nor detest His correction; for whom the LORD loves He corrects, just as a father the son in whom he delights.

PROVERBS 3:11–12

The rod and rebuke give wisdom, but a child left to himself brings shame to his mother.

PROVERBS 29:15

Correct your son, and he will give you rest; yes, he will give delight to your soul.

PROVERBS 29:17

Because the sentence against an evil work is not executed speedily, therefore the heart of the sons of men is fully set in them to do evil.

ECCLESIASTES 8:11

There are some tough-sounding words in those verses: chastening, reproof, correction, sentencing, the rod. And there are comforting words in those same verses too: nurture and admonition of the Lord, love, delight, wisdom, and rest.

Yes, these verses do contain an interesting mixture of words. I want to take note of the fact that this surely is not the picture of a mean, cruel, unkind adult venting his wrath on his children. On the contrary, these Scriptures paint a picture of someone who is familiar with the Word of God, approaching a child whom he loves and delights in. His objective is to teach and to guide.

PHYSICAL PUNISHMENT?

When does physical punishment happen? That is the question you have been waiting for me to answer, is it not? This question must be viewed within the framework of the limits you have given. The child should not be taken by surprise. Instead, the limits should clearly define what is expected and what will be the results of not meeting those expectations. As I see it, pressure should move from weak to strong—and only as needed:

1. If there is any doubt about a child's knowledge of the limits, then, of course, instruction is in order.
2. Making something available that would reward a child may help.
3. If there is deliberate dawdling or loafing, some reproof may work.
4. Depriving a child of something he prefers may help.
5. Taking a young child by the hand and helping her pick up an object is still greater pressure.
6. Spanking may help.

As I see it, spanking should be reserved for a defiant, rebellious, conscious challenge of your leadership. It should settle the question of who is in charge. In his book *Dare to Discipline,* Dr. Dobson says that nothing brings a parent and child closer together than a parent winning decisively when defiantly challenged. I agree. Nothing builds respect for you like confirming your leadership.

A firm swat on the bottom will also help center a child's attention. How much pressure do you use? As little as possible, but enough to get his attention and inspire him to comply.

But let me issue a word of caution here. Pressure should be applied by kind hands and only used when necessary.

It is most important to be clear on this: If you love your children, you will chasten them. However, a parent who has lost his temper should never chasten his child. The chastisement should only be for the child's good—for the child's personal development. It should never be an expression of the parent's anger.

Understandably, chastisement is never a happy time for either the parent or the child, but in the long run it will help the child to be happy. To be effective, fair and well-balanced chastisement should be well planned and well intended.

When our children were preschoolers, they unknowingly taught me a lesson about the relationship between perception of pain and the climate of chastisement. I would lie on my back, put a child up on my feet, and boost him through the air so that he landed on the couch. The children just loved it. This was a nightly ritual at our house. But one night one of the children missed the couch and came crashing to the floor. I thought the child would be injured, but much to my surprise, the child jumped up, eyes shining, and said, "Do it again, Daddy."

The other children added, "Do it to me too."

I did an experiment that night and deliberately threw the children (relatively softly, of course) on the floor. They roughhoused with each other and I even slapped their hands.

They loved it and wanted more. A few days later, however, one of the children did something wrong. I grabbed the child's hand and slapped it with less force than I had several nights before. The child cried as if his heart would break.

What was the difference between the two nights? It was the emotional climate. A few nights before, both of us had been in a good mood, having a good time. Now the mood was different. Generally speaking, the child who is spanked by a parent who is responding out of a loving spirit will react much more to the emotional pain of being punished and much less to the minor discomfort of a swat on the behind or slap on the hand.

Some people think that if they never lay a hand on their children, they have not been cruel to them. Let's take a second look at this thinking. Most know of the pain of sharp words. You might be a parent who has determined to never spank your child, but you freely take well-chosen sentences and let him have it. Words can sometimes hurt a child much more than a spanking that comes from a loving heart ever could.

Silence can also be hurtful. Are there times in your home when no one says a word? Yes, no one is laying a hand on anyone else, but there is just silence, quietness—the child is being ignored, tuned out, and rejected. Such silence can be more painful than a spanking that is intended to help children pay serious attention to the limits that have been set before them.

Discipline and spanking need not imply a lack of love. As I noted earlier in this book, the spirit in which punishment is given makes the difference. The use of physical punishment need not mean a lack of love. It just gets the child's attention. Avoiding physical punishment does not always mean love is present. In fact, many people abhor spanking, because they are angry when they do it; but then because their anger goes unchecked, they wound their children with harmful words or silent rejection.

As noted earlier in the book, after a child has been corrected, he will be looking for clues as to whether or not you have now withdrawn your love. It is imperative for your child to know—before, during, and after any punishment—that your love for him remains strong, steadfast, and sure.

ATTITUDES

Attitude and viewpoint are so very important when a parent assesses consequences—good or bad—for the child's actions.

I remember my team physician in high school. He had examined me many times and knew perfectly well that my physical condition was good.

Then one day I hobbled into his office with a sore knee that had swelled up so much that it filled my pant leg and hurt so that I could not straighten it.

Keep in mind that he knew I was in good shape otherwise. Even so, he did not even mention my good physical condition. He was only interested in my sore knee. "Put it on this table and straighten it out."

Man, that was excruciating pain.

Next, he began to thump it. He wanted to find out where it hurt the worst. So he thumped the sorest spot a few more times just to make sure he had located it.

Then he smiled at me and said, "I've got to lance it."

He was humming to himself as he walked away, and when he returned—with a knife in his hand—he was smiling. "This will hurt," he said.

Sure enough, he cut my knee open, lanced it, and sewed it back up—and he was smiling and jovial the whole time. Then he said to me, obviously pleased with himself, "There—now you'll get better."

At the time I was in horrible pain. As a matter of fact, I had never felt such intense pain before. Yet the doctor was telling me that things were going to be all right. And smiling about it! My knee did get better. Isn't it strange how surgeons are some of the most highly respected and highly paid people in our communities? We do not necessarily like what they do, but we like the results—even if pain is involved. My team doctor was not cruel when he cut into my knee: He was compassionately helpful.

Parenthood is sometimes like being a surgeon. Whether or not our children like what we do is not what is important. The results of what we do must be what guide us. Consequences that are assessed from a heart of love will produce bountiful results in the future. Do not be afraid to make sure that your children experience the consequences—good and bad—of their behavior.

THE MYSTERY OF IT ALL...PERSEVERANCE

Solving the mystery of how to work with your children lies in responding to resistance, giving help, respecting one another, supervising the children's activities, and setting and enforcing limits.

You must have a plan and then throw all you have into following that plan...making sure the consequences for the child's behavior are in place.

Several years ago, a couple was having a real problem with their thirteen-year-old son. He was flunking in school, fighting with his teachers, sassing his parents, and fighting with his neighbors.

His parents tried everything. First, they ignored him. Then they praised him. Then they rewarded him. Then they reasoned with him, lectured him, and withheld dessert. Then they took his bike away, made him stay in the house, and spanked him.

Nothing seemed to work. The parents kept after the boy—while they constantly showed real affection and approval of the boy himself. They also prayed for patience and grace. This went on for six months and nothing seemed to change. Then, just as mysteriously as the behavior had begun, the boy began to change for the better.

In the past, the boy had been condemned and censored by teachers, neighbors, and Sunday school teachers. Two years later, the same boy was a top student, on the football team, and praised and admired by the coach, classmates, teachers, and neighbors.

This is the perfect picture of a dedicated, good-natured set of parents seeking to train a child in the way he should go. They realized it was a twenty-year process. Their concern was the process, not the decisions and appearances of the moment. They had to hang loose, trust God, and act by faith.

TRUST YOURSELF

Often when parents talk about their children who are in trouble, I ask them what they think they should have done differently. In nearly every case, if the parents had done what they thought they should have done, they would have done what I would have recommended.

I am mentioning this to highlight the fact that many parents do not have confidence in their own abilities. Rather than being paralyzed by fear and insecurity, they need to look to God's Word as the source and inspiration for their plan. From there, they need to trust themselves as they proceed with confident expectation of good results.

Any two dedicated parents who are running the family household as gracious and responsive parents, walking by the Word and Spirit of God on a daily and lifelong basis, will make sound judgments. Remember, the primary goal is to train the children up in the way they should go. You have twenty years to mellow and mature. Pray that you will live your life in such a way that your children will grow up wanting to serve the God you serve.

12

A BAKER'S DOZEN...FOR PARENTS

"HEY, I HAVE HEARD THAT ONE BEFORE!" WE HOPE THAT is what you will say as you read this chapter, for it is time to look back at the last eleven chapters and remind ourselves of the principles in this book. As you reconsider these principles, consider them more than just words—consider them as thirteen friends who can help make parenthood more enjoyable.

WITH A LITTLE HELP...
FROM THIRTEEN FRIENDS!

1. Confident expectation—based on the assumption that you are doing or requiring something you believe is worthwhile and in the best interests of your child. If you are convinced of this, you will have enough conviction to see it through.

2. You need help from a source outside yourself—God Himself, through Jesus Christ. I have good news for you if you have been living this statement: "If only my child would behave, then I would be happy." The good news is that happiness comes from God, and neither people nor circumstances can interfere with your joy if God is truly who you look to as being your source of abundant life.

    Remember what the Bible says: "But the fruit of the Spirit is love, joy peace, longsuffering, kindness, goodness, faithfulness, gentleness, self-control. Against such there is no law" (Galatians 5:22–23).

3. Parenthood is partnership. The basic job of parenthood is to design a harness that both parents will wear. In light of this, parents should heed Paul's admonition in Philippians 2:2–3: "Then make my joy complete by being like-minded, having the same love, being one in spirit and purpose. Do nothing out of selfish ambition or vain conceit, but in humility consider others better than yourselves" (NIV).

4. But the nature of human nature is to go your own way: "All we like sheep have gone astray; we have turned, every one, to his own way; and the LORD has laid on Him the iniquity of us all" (Isaiah 53:6).

Whether the dynamics involve your partner or your children or your best friend, strain on the relationship will surface at the point of trying to make decisions together.

5. The husband is the president—and is responsible for making sure he and his wife wear the harness they both designed. Husbands and wives should submit to each other in the fear of God, and wives should submit to their husbands as unto the Lord (see Ephesians 5:21–22).

6. The wife is the executive vice president—and usually the leading expert on the home and family. In her role, she needs to have clear-cut responsibilities with appropriate authority.

7. Both parents must be effectively busy. Proverbs 31 describes the talents of a woman. Both parents should be using their talents. Jesus gives a formula for greatness: "'Whoever desires to become great among you shall be your servant'" (Mark 10:43).

8. Parenthood is a daily effort over a period of twenty years. It is a long haul. Longsuffering, with joy, is a fruit of the Spirit.

9. Setting limits is the parents' responsibility. The boundaries and rules (called limits in this book) are the results of decisions made by the adults. While the older child may contribute recommendations, the final decisions are not made by the child.

    Setting limits is a family plan, one that keeps changing. Therefore, many meetings between parents are necessary to maintain an up-to-date, reasonable plan. Remember that the purpose of your plan is to train up your children in the way they should go, so that when they are old, they will not depart from it (see Proverbs 22:6).

10. Resistance to the plan is a natural occurrence...so your children will need your help. The nature of human nature is to go your own way. Children have a plan of their own, so resistance to your plan should be expected. They need a good-humored mother who appreciates the contest and enjoys it, and a good-humored father who backs her up and steps in to help. Here are some tools to help you overcome their resistance:

    a. redirecting a child's behavior or attention
    b. giving physical help as needed
    c. giving more help than needed
    d. preparing in advance
    e. using pressure—from weak to strong

    The use of these tools is a matter of making Spirit-controlled decisions.

11. Children need supervision. Setting limits, dealing with resistance, and giving help: Put them together and give them a name and that name is supervision. To make all of these components work together for the benefit of the child, long-term commitment to the same limits and personal involvement are required. You have to believe in your plan!

12. The truth about consequences. Choices have their consequences...good or bad, comfortable or uncomfortable, pleasant or painful. Announcing the consequences for a child's choices and making them happen is a crucial part of teaching children. They must learn the principles expressed in Galatians 6:7: "Do not be deceived, God is not mocked; for whatever a man sows, that he will also reap."

13. Trust your own instincts. I will put my hopes on the judgment of any parents who walk in the Spirit, respect one another and their children, and are committed to a mutually agreeable and mutually binding plan.

CONCLUSION

Parenthood is a full-time job. To qualify, you need to be a person of inner peace—the peace that passes understanding is given by God and is evidenced in the unexpected, unprepared for, unwanted twists and turns of life. This inner peace, then, makes life a fascinating, pleasant journey, wherever it may lead.

To be successful, parenthood requires a partnership of two people who are dedicated to the task of blending their bodies, souls, and spirits into a unit committed to serving God and pleasing Him.

Parenthood requires an acceptance of the task, the desire to understand it, and the willingness to be as diligent in preparation and performance as the most accomplished artist, businessperson, or professional person.

Conflicts and problems will arise, but these can lead you to ever higher levels of accomplishment as God demonstrates His power through the adversity. To identify problems and solve them is to find success. To cover them up or pretend they are not there is to taste defeat. Each partner, as a dedicated servant of God, should be ready and willing to fulfill his or her responsibility in any decision or task.

There is nothing magical or accidental about living a life of happiness, peace, and joy. Building a happy family requires abiding in Christ. There is nothing easy or automatic about it.

Guiding children implies a purpose and a goal. You need to know where you are going. You need to assume responsibility for influencing your children. Your influence for good, or for ill, will probably have more effect on the lives of your children than anything else they will encounter. You must work hard to make learning wholesome and effective for your children.

Parenthood is a twenty-year-long developmental process. If you do your work well, your children will leave to attend to their own careers and families. Therefore, it is important for parents to be effective partners who are interdependent and remain close to one another.

As a couple, you will reach your later years just as you started—only the two of you facing a new and glorious life together. Train your family with this goal in mind: It will be a joyful day for you, with memories of happy years gone by, when the day comes for you to say "Godspeed" to your children as they begin to plan for their own families.

Then you can look ahead with keen anticipation because you have trained your children in the way they should go (see Proverbs 22:6). Then you and your partner can look deep into each other's united souls and anticipate the time when the risen Lord will say to you, "Well done, thou good and faithful servant." Meanwhile, with mutual consent you can say, "Lord, bring on our new life together and let us make it a fruitful one for the glory of God."

LET'S HAVE A BALL!

The most consistent theme in this entire book is that parenthood can be fun. Parenthood should be a twenty-year adventure.

I want to encourage you to center your life and your household in God, and personalize into your life these principles for knitting your family together in love, faith, and joy. And have fun together as you grow up in the Lord Jesus Christ.

Yes, it is God's will for you to enjoy and cherish your children and your lives of abundance together!

Printed in the United States
by Baker & Taylor Publisher Services